C L A S S I C
YACHT INTERIORS

CLASSIC
YACHT INTERIORS
BY JILL BOBROW & DANA JINKINS

Concepts Publishing

To R.P.

Library of Congress Cataloging in Publication Data

Bobrow, Jill, 1951-
    Classic yacht interiors.

    1. Yachts and yachting—Furniture, equipment,
etc.   I. Jinkins, Dana, 1950-   . II. Title.
VM331.B66 1982   623.8'223   82-8933
ISBN 0-393-03274-4   AACR2

ISBN 0-393-03274-4

ACKNOWLEDGEMENTS

Published and Written by Jill Bobrow
Conceived, Photographed and Designed by Dana Jinkins
Associate Designer, Production Supervisor: Robert C. Smith
Design Consultant: B. Martin Pedersen
Associate Editor: William J. Stedman
Copy Editor: Jerry Fales
Technical Advisor: Kenneth Mitchnick
Accommodation and Sail Plan Illustrator: James Eastland
Endpaper Illustration: Peter Carr
Boat Renderings: Cynthia Kaul

Printing: Dai Nippon Printing Company, Ltd., Tokyo, Japan
Paper: 86 lb. Glossy Coated
Typography: Empire Coldtype Inc., New York
Type Styles: Century Expanded and Helvetica Light

Concepts Publishing
P.O. Box 504
Westbrook Ct. 06498
Distributed by W. W. Norton & Company, Inc.
500 Fifth Avenue, New York, N.Y. 10110

Publication of this book was made possible by the encouragement, support, and help from our friends.

Firstly, we would like to express our gratitude to all of the boatowners, skippers, and crew who welcomed us aboard, answered all of our questions, and allowed us to take photographs.

Since this is our first book and first attempt at publishing, we greatly relied on advice from professionals and friends in the business; Sam Lovell and Spencer Smith at Book of the Month Club, Eric Swenson and Jim Mairs at W.W. Norton, and Kaoru Shinzaki at Dai Nippon Printers.

And although they may not enjoy being grouped together, we are appreciative of the time and consultation afforded us from Jeff Hammond at *Boating Magazine*, Oliver Moore, Dan and Jerry Fales at *Motor Boating & Sailing* Magazine, and Keith Taylor at *Sail Magazine*.

The design firm Jonson, Pedersen, Hinrichs & Shakery came to our rescue during the production crunch and offered us a space to work in—we are thankful for all the drawers, drafting tables, wax machine, etc. Martin Pedersen and Randell Pearson were always accessible for their opinions, and Bob Smith stayed many a night ever-ready with the X-ACTO blade. And thanks to his wife Debbie for being understanding and assisting on our cover.

Talking about space, we are also thankful to our numerous ports in a storm; thanks to LiLi Townsend, Adele DeCruz, Patti Goodman, Paul Hecht, and Marla Mitchnick for their New York apartments...to Alan Gowell and Melanie Jones for their division of Concepts Publishing in Martha's Vineyard...to Bill and Karla Bove for their division of Concepts Publishing in St. Martin...to Nolly Simmons for his division of Concepts Publishing in Bequia...to Robert and Marty Jinkins for their division of Concepts Publishing in Wichita, Kansas...and to Hersh and Raelea Bobrow for their division of Concepts Publishing in Westbrook, Connecticut.

We had many nautical advisors; we would like to give special thanks to William E. Peterson, of Peterson Custom Yachts in Damariscotta, Maine and to William M. Peterson of Murray G. Peterson Ass., South Bristol, Maine for their input as naval architects and designers.

We would also like to thank K.T. Stewart for some preliminary typing and Barbara Mitchell of Integrity Business in Sarasota for a rush job on the rest — Jerry Fales for last minute copy editing—Jim Eastland for making the deadline—Adam Engle and Richard Gitlin for legal consultation—the accounting firm of Bobrow & Bobrow who are about to put order into our lives—also Dana's babysitters; Cynthia, John and Natasha, without whom there would never have been time to get this book done—and to Jordan Danielle herself for being so patient with our late night production schedule—to John Signaigo for advice and giving us a good deal on photographic equipment. And special thanks to Jimmy Wallen for his belief in a second printing. Oh yes, and thanks to Leonard, Paul, Tickles, Bradley, and Stan for use of their dinghies. And thanks to Linda Lally for helping choose our title.

We would like to thank the readers for putting up with this acknowledgement list—we'd also like to thank all of our seagypsy friends and all the people we love—and particular thanks to Bill and Kenny for their tolerance, patience, support, endurance, and everlasting love....The end.

Soon to be a major motion picture!

CONTENTS

Preface   IX

Introduction   1

Feature Boats   2-132

A Copy   82′ Broward Motor Yacht   2

Aquila   42′ Sparkman & Stephens
                      Yawl   6

Belle Aventure   95′ Fife Ketch   10

Blue Diamond   70′ River Cruiser   14

Buxom   33′ Tahiti Ketch   16

Charlotte Ann   62′ Schooner   18

Chesapeake   40′ Sparkman & Stephens   20

Cotton Blossom   72′ Fife Yawl   22

Cyprae   59′ Malabar X Schooner   24

Deliverance   96′ Eldridge McGuinness
                      Schooner   26

Edna   100′ Dutch Luger   30

Enchanta   67′ Alden Yawl   34

Escapade   80′ Rhodes Yawl   38

Eyola   75′ Brigantine Schooner   40

Firebird   85′ Sparkman & Stephens
                      Ketch   42

Fish Hawk   63′ Alden Cutter   44

Freedom   12 meter: 1980 America's
                      Cup Winner   46

Galia   80′ Bermuda Ketch   48

Gleam   67′ 12 meter Sloop   52

Isla de Ibiza   96′ Gaff Schooner   54

Janette   118′ Williamson/
                      Bannenberg Motor
                      Yacht   56

Jens Juhl   120′ Baltic Trader Ketch   58

Kialoa III   79′ Sparkman & Stephens
                      Racing Sloop   62

Lene Marie   106′ Baltic Trader   64

Lindø   125′ Three Masted Baltic
                      Trader   66

Nirvana   65′ Alden Yawl   70

Now Voyager   68′ Dermit McGuinness
                      Motor Yacht   74

Ondine   79′ Briton Chance Ketch   76

Palawan   68′ Sparkman & Stephens
                      Ketch   78

Papillon   57′ William Tripp Yawl   80

Pigalle   48′ Custom French Sloop   82

Rebel   66′ McCurdy & Rhodes
                      Ketch   84

Royono   85′ Alden Yawl   86

Rugosa   59′ Nat Herreshoff
                      New York 40   88

Sandpiper   35′ Winthrop Warner Ketch   92

Satori   75′ Gaff Schooner   96

Scotch Mist   95′ Wm. Garden
                      Motorsailer   100

Sea Cloud   353′ Stevens & Cox
                      Schooner   104

Serendy   56′ Catamaran Sloop   106

Silver Heels   41′ Murray Peterson
                      Schooner   108

Souqui   79′ Dutch River Barge   110

Southerly   55′ Sparkman & Stephens
                      Ketch   112

Starbound   68′ Auxiliary Ketch   114

The Sting   Freedom 40   116

Tabor Boy   92′ Training Schooner   118

Tantra Schooner   80′ Custom Schooner   120

Tar Baby   60′ Alden Schooner   124

Ticonderoga   72′ Herreshoff Ketch   126

Vanda   93′ Stowe Ketch   128

Victoria   72′ Herreshoff Ketch   130

Volcano   62′ Frers Sloop   132

Main Saloons   134-148

Eudroma	64' Ketch	134
Cyrano	77' Motorsailer	134
Taipi II	45' French Schooner	135
Tantra	75' Motor Sailer Ketch	135
Blue Jacket	52' Ocean Racing Yawl	136
Raanga	72' Steel Schooner	136
Alkyone	Swan 57	136
Wind Dancer	Cherubini 44	137
Free Spirit	76' Cutter	137
New Horizons	60' Ketch	137
Active	43' Murray Peterson Schooner	138
Elinor	118' Baltic Trader	138
Galadriel	37' Steel Yawl	139
Freedom	60' Nova Scotia Schooner	139
Adventure	121' Windjammer Schooner	139
Plumbelly	25' Bequia built boat	139
Shearwater	62' Alden Ketch	140
Wrestler	1926 Tug Boat	140
Mary Day	83' Windjammer Schooner	140
Bride of Gastonia	45' Seth Persson	141
Athena	80' Custom Ketch	141
Viking	40' Cruising Ketch	142
Alegria	64' Rhodes Ketch	142
Linda	48' Baltic Trader	143
Argyll	58' Sparkman & Stephens Yawl	143
Mattie	Windjammer Schooner	143
Sherpa	60' Custom French Catamaran	144
Quicksilver	47' Norm Cross Trimaran	144
Paradise	50' Gulfstar	144
Vixen	New York 40	144
Stardust	47' Greiger	145
Lusty	62' Wm. Tripp Ketch	145
Malu Kai	Irwin 52' Ketch	145
Sayonara	118' Custom Yawl	146
Zozo	54' Taiwan Ketch	146
Christiana	47' Colin Archer	147
White Wing	50' Alden Sloop	147
Grym III	52' Ted Hood Ketch	147
Enchanta	67' Alden Yawl	147

Berths and Cabins   148-153

Sayonara	118' Custom French Yacht	148,149
Felicidad	D. Peterson 45' Sloop	150
Zozo	54' Taiwan Ketch	150
Alegria	64' Rhodes Ketch	151
Quicksilver	47' Norm Cross Trimaran	151
Zaida	63' Alden Cutter	151
Eudroma	64' Ketch	152
Vagabond	52' Wm. Garden Ketch	152
Linda	48' Baltic Trader	152
Sleuth	54' P. J. Racing Sloop	152
Blue Diamond	70' River Cruiser	153
Karena	Morgan 51	153
Water Lily	Wm. Hand Motorsailer	153
Scotch Mist	95' Wm. Garden Motorsailer	153

Heads   154-155

Argyll	58' Sparkman & Stephens Yawl	154
Eyola	75' Brigantine Schooner	155
Enchanta	67' Alden Yawl	155
Vanda	93' Stowe Ketch	155
Mary Day	83' Windjammer Schooner	155
Ysas	63' Sparkman & Stephens	156
Galia	80' Bermuda Ketch	156
Souqui	79' Dutch river barge	156
Free Spirit	76' Cutter	157
Taipi II	45' French Schooner	157

Navigation Areas and Cockpits — 160-161

Premlata	33' Quoddy Pilot	158
Argyll	58' Sparkman & Stephens	158
Water Lily	Wm. Hand Motorsailer	159
Felicidad	D. Peterson 45	159
Windsong	58' Custom Ketch	160
Voyager	Alden Schooner	160
Lusty	62' Wm. Tripp Ketch	160
Galia	80' Bermuda Ketch	161
Linda	48' Baltic Trader	161

Galleys — 162-179

Sea Cloud	353' Schooner	163
Jan Pamela II	141' Dutch Motor Yacht	164
Paradise	Gulfstar 50	166
Free Spirit	76' Cutter	166
Rachel and Ebenezer	105' Schooner	167
Viking	40' Crusing Ketch	167
Vixen	New York 40	167
Amoeba	64' Schooner	168
Miss Caroline	Westsail 42	168
Sleuth	54' P. J. Racing Sloop	169
Aquila	42' Sparkman & Stephens Yawl	169

Ocean Mistral	Ocean 60	170
Vagabond	54' Taiwan Ketch	170
Whistler	Ocean 71	172
Tivoli	71' Sangermani racer/cruiser	172
Endless Summer	Custom West Indies 46	172
Flying Fifty	70' Uffa Fox Yawl	172
Wind Dancer	Cherubini 44	173
Tiara	63' Motor Sailer Ketch	173
Impulsive	Irwin 52	173
Galadriel	37' Steel Yawl	174
Riki Tiki Tavi	30' Cutter	174
Adventure	121' Windjammer Schooner	175
Amigo	54' Custom Yawl	175
Leander	39' Casey Cutter	176
Slipaway	28' Bahamian Sloop	176
Zingara	30' English Cutter	177
MYA	50' Concordia Schooner	177
Elinor	117' Baltic Trader	177
Water Pearl	Schooner being built on the beach in Bequia. Owned by: Bob Dylan and Chris Bowman	178-179

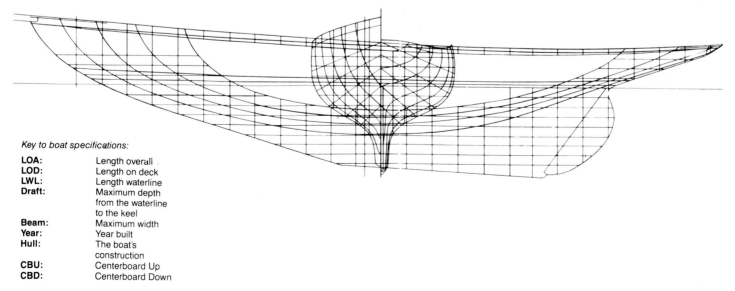

Key to boat specifications:

LOA:	Length overall
LOD:	Length on deck
LWL:	Length waterline
Draft:	Maximum depth from the waterline to the keel
Beam:	Maximum width
Year:	Year built
Hull:	The boat's construction
CBU:	Centerboard Up
CBD:	Centerboard Down

PREFACE

Dana and I are two seafaring gypsies who share a love for boats, having lived and worked on a variety of them. Our mutual home base for years was the island of Bequia, a magical spot, nine miles south of St. Vincent in the Grenadines. Bequia is only accessible by sea. The protected harbor, Admiralty Bay is usually replete with vessels from all over the world. This tiny international crossroads attracts both passersby and more permanent residents. We watched many boats tack into the harbor and never tired of musing about who was on board, where they came from and what the boat looked like below.

Dana conceived the idea of a book on boat interiors. A friend gave her some money to buy film. She photographed at least a dozen boats and then contacted me. We hadn't seen each other in a year. Dana's enthusiasm was infectious. I became involved immediately.

Together we set out in search of boats that were beautiful, famous, representative of a type or unique. We borrowed dinghies and roamed around countless harbors. We knocked on hulls, relying on our instincts, word of mouth and local knowledge. Either we photographed right then and there or we made a date and time to come back when the boat was sure to be prepared. Of course, our appointments didn't preclude unscheduled engine problems with the main saloon torn apart and tools scattered everywhere. On occasion we washed dishes in the galley or got out the Brasso to spruce up a fireplace.

In our naïveté, we had long ago determined that it would be fun to publish ourselves. We were so close to the whole project we couldn't imagine relinquishing any part of it to an established publishing house. Nonetheless about half way through, we panicked and decided to look for help. After months of making presentations and sending out our "unsolicited manuscript" we discovered that since we were willing to do everything, we might as well go with our initial instinct. We set out to raise money for production and printing. In between shoots and boat interviews, we educated ourselves about paper, color separations, typesetting, camera ready mechanicals with photostats in place, printing, binding, distribution, promotion, subsidiary sales, etc., etc....

We love boats and want to share our thoughts and ideas about them.

Jill Bobrow

INTRODUCTION

Author Jill Bobrow and photographer Dana Jinkins have assembled in this volume the most broad ranging and exciting collection of yacht interiors that I have ever seen. A collectors' item, this book combines a labor of love with an unusually high level of craftsmanship and reproduction. That is what makes *Classic Yacht Interiors* so special.

To a large degree the great age of yachting is over. Once scores of boat yards dotted the American and European coasts, each building only a few exquisite custom boats a year. Today they have all but disappeared. in their place are high volume production fiberglass manufacturers building scores of boats, each very much like the other, particularly below decks. It was in the cabinetry and wood joinerwork where craftsmanship and man hours were lavished and that is precisely where the art of yacht building has been compromised since.

Classic Yacht Interiors is more than a fine collection of yacht interiors. It is a record of a passing era, a time when designers and builders spent as much effort on the finer detail of the accommodations as they do now on hull shape, speed, and where to put the genoa track.

For over two years, Bobrow and Jinkins traveled extensively, seeking out these very special yachts. And who among us has not seen vessels like them from afar and wondered what they must be like below? Now we are given an opportunity on these pages; an invitation aboard and a peek below. You find yourself saying, "This is the way it should be done!" or, "Why don't they do that anymore?" And you marvel at all of the good ideas that make things handy, or easy, or more comfortable and inviting— little things that you instinctively know evolved slowly over the years by people who spent their lives on boats.

With each passing year there will be fewer of these great yachts calling on the salty ports of America and the world. *Classic Yacht Interiors* will keep their memory bright for a long time and give future generations a benchmark with which to judge yachts in the next century.

My first impression of this book is how wonderful it is to be presented with photographic descriptions of interior arrangements of so many yachts, diverse in size and opulence and varying fifty or more years in age. Being presented in color photographs, excellent photographs indeed, taken from sites which were very well chosen to give the reader a great feeling of presence, the value of this book as a reference work to yacht designers or builders is immense and to my knowledge an innovation.

Because of rather confined spaces, photographing yacht interiors is a very difficult and demanding task. The photography in this book is unique. The photographer used considerable skill in selecting shooting sites and angles which resulted in unusually good interior pictures.

To anyone contemplating the construction of a yacht or the decoration or re-decoration of one, this book will be of infinite value.

This book gives a reader a wonderful opportunity to "visit" and vicariously enjoy life aboard many yachts from many countries. The reader on these "visits" has a wide choice of life styles aboard because of the range in yacht sizes and different degrees of luxury depicted in the fine photography of the interiors.

In this day and age of synthetic plastics and man made fabrics, it is refreshing to see how master craftsmen used wood, not only for structural elements, but as is so beautifully illustrated in this book, for decorative trim, panels and cabinetry. The photography brings out, vividly, the joiners' skill and artistry in their use of grain, color and texture of various woods to enhance the designers' concepts in their planning for play of light and shadow.

This fine book is not only useful from a practical view but will also give much pleasure to the casual reader because of its portrayal of beauty found in the design and construction of ordinary, functional elements.

Jeff Hammond
Publisher/Boating Magazine

William E. Peterson
Yacht Builder

A COPY

Type:	Motor Yacht
LOA:	82'
Beam:	18'6"
Draft:	6'
Designer/ Builder:	Broward, Broward City, Florida
Year:	1979
Hull:	Aluminum
Power:	Twin 675-hp GM 12-71 turbocharged diesels
Aux. Electrical Supply:	Twin 30,000 watt Westerbeke Generators

Photograph by Broward Marine

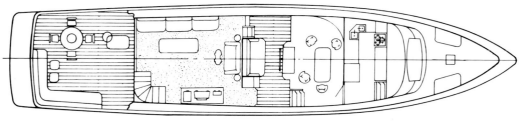

We found *A Copy* nesting among the other "gold platers" at Pier 66 in Ft. Lauderdale. She is an 82' custom-built Broward. Not a floating condominium, *A Copy* has a cruising range of 2,000 miles. Owner Herb Chambers, of Old Lyme, Ct. can leave his executive pressures on shore and go voyaging in style.

A Copy's interior was handsomely designed by Repco of Hartford. The aft sundeck is the most used area on the boat. There is an "L-shaped" lounging settee covered in gray velour on the starboard side: soft, cool and comfortable for bare legs. The port side sports a luncheon table, with a wet bar and icemaker conveniently nearby. The sundeck is separated from the main saloon by Plexiglas doors. The main saloon is very contemporary, with a built-in entertainment center, a jigsaw patterned beige and brown carpet, chrome lamps, and a mirrored bulkhead dividing it from the dining room.

The use of leather for the couches adds a kind of rugged opulence—somewhat reminiscent of Abercrombie and Fitch. (Perhaps it is the life-size sheep in the main saloon). The dining room is incredibly dramatic. The glass table and elegant high back chairs shimmer in the reflection of yet another mirrored bulkhead. The twin generators provide ample power for the deep freezers, electric stove, d/w, garbage disposal, etc. The cabins below deck accommodate six guests and three crew. We were struck by the master head: mirrors, vanity lights, and a gold plated sink!

AQUILA

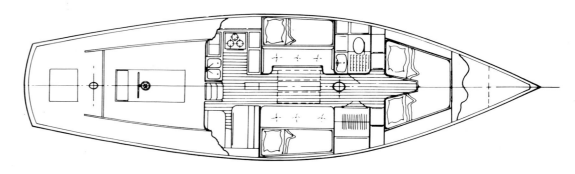

Type:	Yawl
LOA:	42'7"
Beam:	12'
Draft:	CBU: 4½';
	CBD: 7½'
Builder:	Tore Yard, Gambly, Sweden
Designer:	Sparkman & Stephens
Year:	1957
Hull:	Double planked mahogany; stainless steel floors and mast step

Photograph by Randy Gurley

*A*quila, an exquisitely conceived and crafted boat, is a sister ship to the famous *Finisterre*. Designed as a cruiser/racer, she has sailed in Scandinavia, the Mediterranean, New England, and the Caribbean.

Built with a conventional layout for an aft cockpit boat, her last owner refitted her in a fashion that yields more efficient use of the (always) limited space. Her aft galley, which spanned both sides of the companionway, is now confined to the port side. The large icebox that was on the starboard side aft has been converted into a chart table and navigation area. The icebox was replaced by a more conveniently located Adler-Barbour refrigeration system.

The main saloon is paneled in Honduras mahogany. The settees here and the bunks in the forepeak have been newly upholstered in Java print fabric from St. Martin. They are sewn like contour sheets and fitted over sturdier duck canvas.

Hand-painted Mexican tiles are used on horizontal surfaces throughout the boat. They add a special touch of creativity to a traditional interior.

Decor is sometimes discounted by "serious" sailors, but just the right touch makes a world of difference.

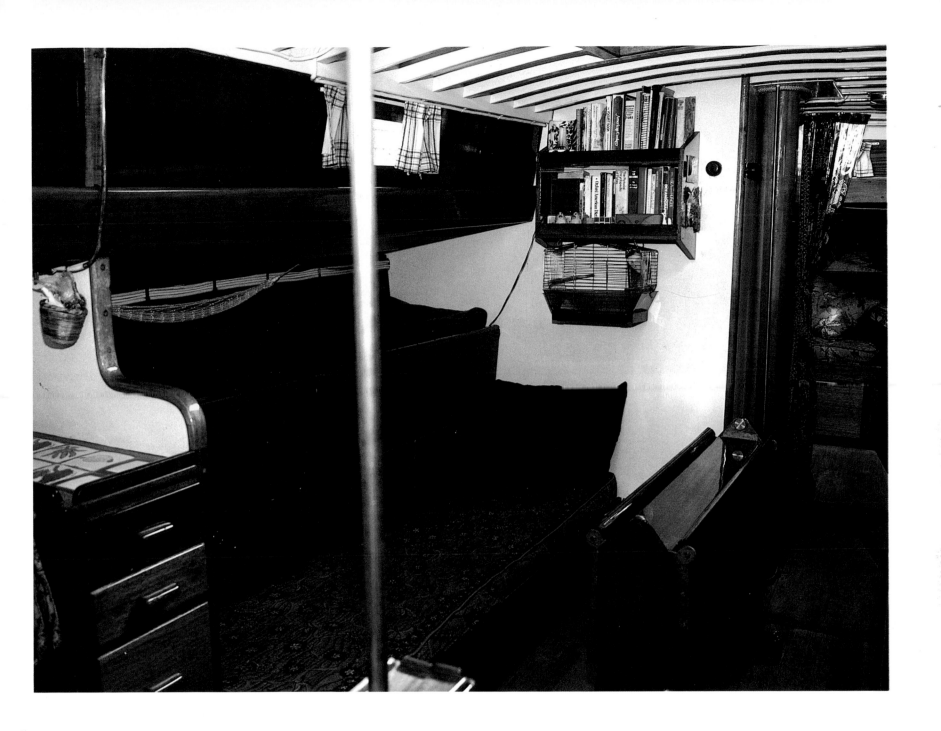

AQUILA

BELLE AVENTURE

Type:	Ketch
LOA:	95'
LOD:	85'
Beam:	17'2"
Draft:	10'7"
Builder/	
Designer:	Wm. Fife & Sons, Fairlie—Scotland
Year:	1929/Renovated 1979—Lloyds
Hull:	Teak over oak frames—bronze fastened

Photographed by Paul Goss

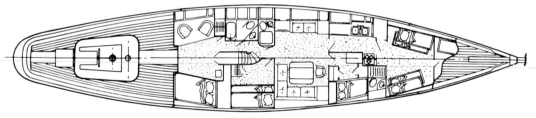

William Fife had a flair for designing very special yachts. *Belle Aventure* is certainly no exception. Built in 1929 as a cruiser/racer, she sailed the short English summers around the Clyde and Hebrides and spent winter and the war years sheltered. Later, she journeyed south, spending twenty years cruising the Mediterranean. Her new owner changed her name from *Eileen* to Belle Aventure and sailed her to the Far East.

In 1979 *Belle Aventure* returned to the Clyde, in order to undergo an extensive refit. Lloyds did a superb job of restoring the original walnut and teak paneling and refurbishing all bright work and bronze. In addition to the cosmetics, she received a new plumbing and electric system, new engine, generator, and a full inventory of sails.

The smooth flush decks and tidy cockpit, with its splendid helm and gleaming binnacle, are an indication of what you'll find below. *Belle Aventure's* interior matches the meticulous grooming of her exterior. From the cockpit you enter the deck saloon

level, where there are two settees and a protected wraparound view. The windows are made from beveled glass. Stairs lead to the main saloon.

There is a settee to port and the dining area to starboard. The most impressive aspect of this room is the wood paneling and the built-in cabinetry and writing desk.

The aft cabin, which lies below the deck house, has a double berth with built-in drawers beneath. A sitting area opposite the bed features two built-in upholstered chairs and a library. The master stateroom also enjoys the luxury of a private head, complete with bathtub. The other cabins provide plenty of stowage, roomy berths, individual reading lamps, and mirrored vanities. Crews quarters and the galley are forward, in keeping with the "upstairs-downstairs" attitude of prewar England. *Belle Aventure* is the ideal charter boat for those who want discreetly elegant decor. Yet, unlike so many opulently appointed charter boats, *Belle Aventure* was built to sail.

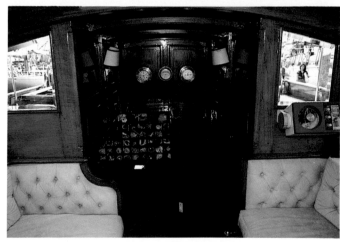

BELLE AVENTURE

BLUE DIAMOND

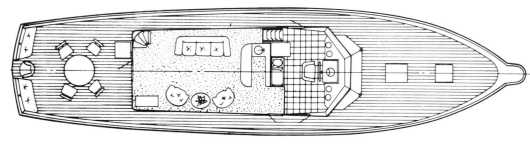

Photograph by Blue Diamond Charters

Type:	Motor Yacht
Length:	70'
Beam:	17'
Draft:	4½'
Designer:	George Frank
Built:	Pleasant Valley, Iowa
Year:	1948
Hull:	Steel

Blue Diamond is a vintage River Cruiser. A long way from the Mississippi River, she is now a charter boat operating out of St. Thomas in the Virgin Islands. It's unusual to see a boat of this sort in the Caribbean. Built with an advanced stabilizing system to prevent rolling, she is like a house afloat.

In 1978, *Blue Diamond* had an extensive refit in Grenada. The most notable changes are the built-in bar and entertainment center, and the highly varnished paneling, all fabricated out of rich mahogany.

The main deck level includes the bridge navigation station, main saloon and the poopdeck. A large, round teak table, which cleverly expands to accommodate 10 for dinner, graces this aft poopdeck. From here a ladder leads to the sundeck and tender stowage area.

The main saloon is a comfortable living room, with wall-to-wall carpeting, large picture windows and homey furniture. An elegant, hand-crafted staircase takes you to the three private staterooms on the lower deck. The master stateroom has a queen size bunk, in addition to a single, and a private head and shower. The curved tiled wall in the head follows the contour of the staircase from the main deck. The two other cabins resemble an old-fashioned sleeper car on a train. Each has a couch that converts to a berth and an athwartships pullman-type hinged bunk, which doubles as a mirror when flush to the wall. These cabins share a head with shower and bathtub.

The galley and crews quarters are separated from the guest cabins by the engine room which extends the full beam of the boat amidships.

Blue Diamond is fully equipped with all of the tricks of the charter trade and more: full entertainment center, fishing equipment, Boston Whaler with outboard, Aquascooters, scuba gear, even skeet equipment. With a wet bar on the sundeck and a full bar and refrigerator in the main saloon, snacks and drinks are conveniently available.

BUXOM II

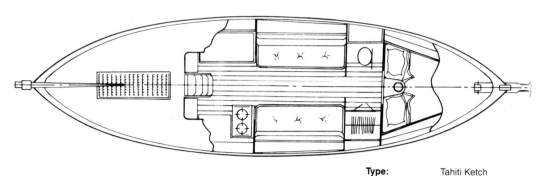

Type:	Tahiti Ketch
LOA:	33'
Beam:	11'
Draft:	5'
Design:	Converted Hanna design; 10% bigger and changed to masthead rig
Built:	Ontario, Canada
Year:	1935
Hull:	Cedar on oak

Maybe it's the baggywrinkle that gives it away. *Buxom* is undeniably a liveaboard boat. Although she looks like she just blew in from the South Seas, *Buxom* has been residing in the Virgin Islands for years. Coziness seems to emanate from this compact little vessel.

The galley counter athwartship acts as a step down from the cockpit, and it can be removed entirely for access to the engine.

The main saloon is very compact. The sleeping quarters are even more so. There is a mast smack dab in the middle of the double bunk in the fo'c' sle. The couple who owns the boat are wooden boat enthusiasts. They have a great sense of humor and the interior reflects their attitude toward fun and make do. The white walls, hammocks of vegetables and sprays of flowers give *Buxom* the air of a carefree summer cottage.

CHARLOTTE ANN

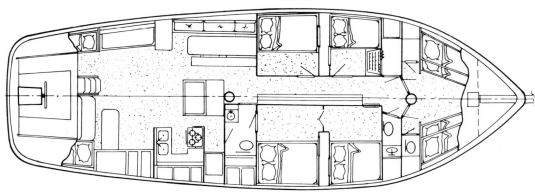

Type:	Schooner
Length:	62'
Beam:	19'
Draft:	Centerboard up: 5½'
Hull:	Wood
Year:	1888 rebuilt 1970
Engine:	GM 671 Diesel
Displacement:	60 long tons
Sail Area:	2,250 sq. ft.

Photograph by John Woodside

Charlotte Ann was originally built in the last century as an oyster dredge. Later in her career she was used without sail as a fishing party boat. In 1970 Charlotte Ann had a rebirth. Her new owners, John and Marge Woodside of Wappingers Falls, New York, reframed, replanked and rebuilt her interior. What had been a hold for oysters became a cabin and deckhouse. The original schooner rig was reinstated. She is a heavy, beamy boat that sails on her bottom and is stable in most any weather.

The main saloon, located aft, paneled in hard pine and mahogany, provides a spacious lounging area. The galley, immediately forward and to starboard, is compact, U-shaped and convenient. The ship's engine is housed in a large galley box whose top is often used for buffet service. The dining is almost picnic table style with long wooden benches.

Four double cabins replete with excellent cabinetwork and two heads are forward. One of the heads has a lovely ceramic basin. The separate shower room for the guest cabin is a good idea.

Charlotte Ann offers a taste of the 19th Century made palatable by 20th Century amenities.

CHESAPEAKE

Type:	Jib-headed mast head Yawl
Length:	40′
LWL:	27′6″
Beam:	11′3″
Draft:	3′11″ centerboard up; cbd: 7′7″
Sail Area:	739 sq. ft.
Built:	Nevins Yacht Yard, City Island, New York
Designer:	Sparkman & Stephens
Year:	1957
Hull:	Wood

Photograph by Rob Patterson

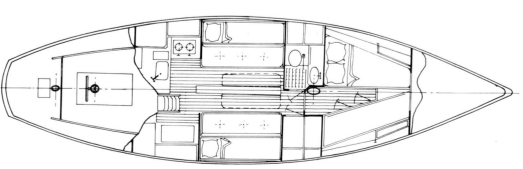

Chesapeake closely resembles her prototype, the famous ocean racing yawl, *Finisterre*. Owners, Rob and Reene Patterson, lived aboard *Chesapeake* for two years, before leaving the more conventional work-a-day world for the Caribbean.

Rather small for the charter business, *Chesapeake* is nonetheless immaculate and comfortable for a party of two or three.

The interior is a bright white with mahogany trim. The sole is teak and holly splined with the holly raised for traction. The settees and pilot berths are nautical blue. A bright red pillow and colorful Mola from the San Blas islands perk up the decor. The only major change to the traditional interior is in the forepeak. The starboard bunk was removed to increase stowage and the port bunk pulls out to create a double.

Both Reene and Rob are U.S. Coast Guard licensed skippers with years of sailing experience. Their boat reflects the tidiness and meticulous care of true sailors.

COTTON BLOSSOM IV

Type:	Yawl
LOA:	71'6"
LWL:	49'6"
Beam:	14'6"
Draft:	9'6"
Builder/	
Designer:	W & R.B. Fife, Fairlie, Scotland
Year:	1926
Hull:	Carvel planked teak on oak
Engine:	Diesel

Photograph by Sandy Brown

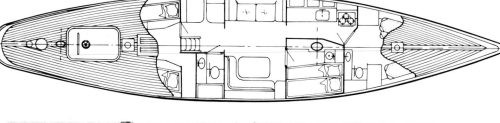

Photograph by Sandy Brown

Cotton Blossom IV, originally built for the Fastnet Race, is one of the most extraordinary racing yachts of all time. She is owned by Dr. Bruce Eissner of Marblehead, Massachusetts, and skippered by Englishman Richard Griffiths. Cotton Blossom is as beautiful as she is fast. Her flush deck, disturbed only by symmetrically ensconced brass winches, is sleek and impressive. Even her small cockpit and helm are distinctive.

Below, her interior bespeaks her Fife tradition. Her layout is conventional, with an owner's stateroom aft, main saloon, forward cabin, galley and crews quarters. The port side forward galley is a trifle small and closed in. Let's just say we would rather be served than serving. The main cabin is exquisite. Incorporating different shades of Honduras mahogany, the paneling is solid and rich feeling. The settees are upholstered in a taupe soft leather, accented by antelope horn buttons. The aft cabin is similarly rich looking, paneled in butternut and mahogany. Fife certainly built boats to last. Cotton Blossom's interior is the original one, and her appearance is timeless.

CYPRAE

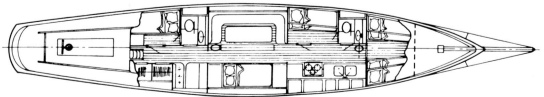

Type:	Malabar X schooner
Length:	59′
Beam:	13′
Draft:	8′1″
Displacement:	33 tons
Builders	Owners: France
Designer:	John G. Alden
Hull:	Steel with iron mesh reinforced with concrete

Cyprae "en français" is a cowry shell. There is a cowry shell inlaid in this boat's exquisite hand-crafted mahogany dining table. Much planning and care went into building *Cyprae*. She is the result of an enormous group effort: brothers, cousins, and a hundred of their closest friends. The five owners are Msrs. J.M. and B. Favreaux, M. St. Sevin, M.J.L. Henry, and M.L.J. Lassus.

They came across the plans for the original *Malabar X* and decided to duplicate her in ferro-cement. (*Malabar X* had won the Bermuda Race two times in the period 1932-1936, maintaining the record for twenty years). The French wanted a beautiful boat that would sail fast and accommodate six charter guests and four crew.

Cyprae is a perfect replica of the original Alden design, the same rig and sail plan. The hull, instead of wood, however, is constructed of steel with iron mesh reinforced concrete. Below, African and Brazilian mahogany and Oregon pine belie her concrete and steel interior.

From the aft cockpit, you descend the stairs and come upon the well-equipped navigation station

directly to starboard. Opposite it are the electric panel, foul weather gear locker and self-contained captain's cabin. Along the companionway is a bookshelf. The books are secured by brass stanchions connected by leather bindings. Then there is a sliding door to enter the main saloon. To starboard is a couch that converts to a double bunk. At the head of the couch is a closet. A curtain pulls out on an overhead hand rail slide from the closet in order to afford this berth some privacy.

There is a recessed well under the main cabin floor that serves as a dustpan. To port is a large semicircular settee and dining table. A bench pulls down from the mast to accommodate more at the table.

The galley is convenient to the main saloon and dining area, and comes with an extra deep double sink. The propane tanks for the stove and hot water heater are stowed on deck. All sorts of French delicacies come out of this well-equipped galley.

Cyprae had enough ideas filtering in with so many people involved in the boat, that a lot of attention was paid to detail.

DELIVERANCE

Our visit aboard the schooner *Deliverance* was an education. Owners David & Lonny Higgins, their two children, and two (sometimes three) crew members live aboard. Seldom have we seen such a well-organized boat. Granted, with 82 feet there is plenty of room to get organized, but this boat is special. We started our tour with David in the pilothouse, which is the navigation area. The chart table is battleship linoleum, a sturdy leathery looking material. Fixed at the bottom is a brass horizontal slot extending the length of the table. This slot enables you to secure the bottom edge of the chart, so that you can lean against it without fraying the edges. The locker opposite the chart table houses the tools. David customized a chest with a slot for each and every tool.

Descending from the pilothouse to the main cabin, immediately to starboard is the aft head, complete with both tub/shower and paneled with bright Italian tiles. Lonny Higgins is an Obstetrician/Gynecologist. However, living aboard and traveling minimizes her office hours. Nonetheless, she maintains the most extensive medicine cabinet we've seen on a yacht. Using Tupperware containers, her medical repertoire is categorized and boldly labeled.

Forward of the head, also on the starboard side, is the master stateroom. A desk folds up from the bulkhead and a neat, curved built-in chair doubles as a laundry bin. Opposite this stateroom on the port side is the children's cabin with upper and lower bunks. A leather trimmed net is rigged to act as lee boards.

Forward of these cabins is the main saloon, which is exquisitely paneled with cherry wood. Lonny has upholstered her settees with Herculon slipcovers that can be removed and washed. The carpet in the main saloon, a comfortable thick pile, is a synthetic non-absorbent fiber called Actionback.

The main saloon has a gimbaled cherry dining table, a brass fireplace that is designed to burn peat, a handsome breakfront, a desk that pulls down on hinges, and a lavish sound system. Tapes are protected from the elements in air-tight containers. In addition to music, Lonny has a collection of medical tapes, to keep updated, and a score of educational tapes. Lonny and David are providing their seven-year-old son with a Calvert School correspondence course.

Forward of the main saloon is the galley. Despite being forward, it's just about perfect. The galley extends the full width of the boat. On the port side

Type:	Schooner
LOA:	96′
LOD:	82′
Beam:	20′
Designer:	Eldridge McGuinness
Builder:	Quincy Adams' yard, Quincy, Massachusetts
Year:	1956
Hull:	African Mahogany on white oak frames
Engine:	GM 6-71 diesel
Total Sail Area:	4,200 sq. ft.

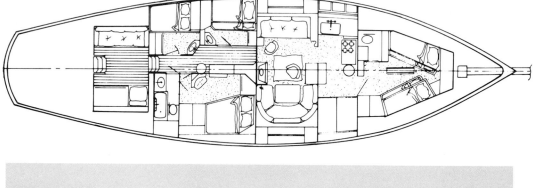

are deep stainless steel double sinks and stainless steel counter space. Rubbermaid mats on the counters prevent dishes from sliding around. Above the sink are cabinets with egg basket-like slots, especially designed for all cups, saucers, plates, etc. Adjacent to the sinks against the forward bulkhead is a Southbend commercial cooking stove, complete with broiler, oven, and storage. There is also a microwave oven. Stainless steel fiddles preclude the necessity of gimbaling the stove as it sits amidships and athwartships. On the bulkhead opposite the stove is another stainless steel counter with cupboards and a pass-through to the main saloon. The pass through leads to the breakfront in the main saloon. To starboard in the galley is a commercial refrigerator-freezer.

The galley is well equipped with bowls and containers especially adapted to boat life. The staples: flour, sugar, salt are kept in canning jars. They twist and seal. Lonny feels the Rosti jars made in Holland are superior to Tupperware for such items. The Rosti bowls come with nonskid bottoms.

To an extent much greater than most, *Deliverance* transcends herself to become nursery, clinic, workshop, school and home.

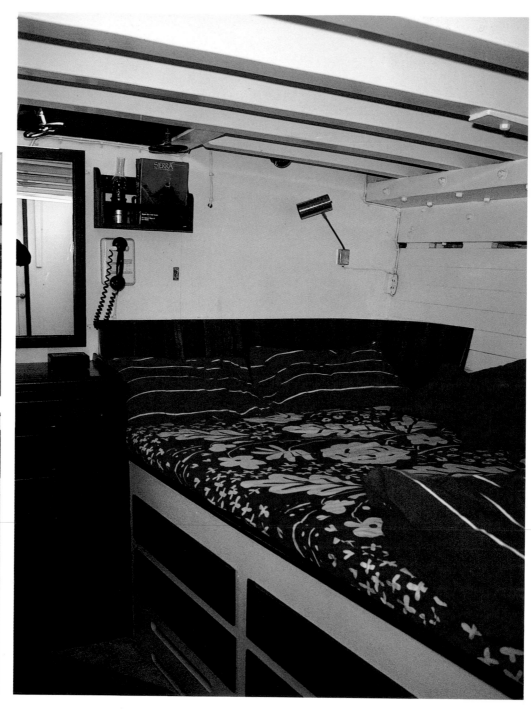

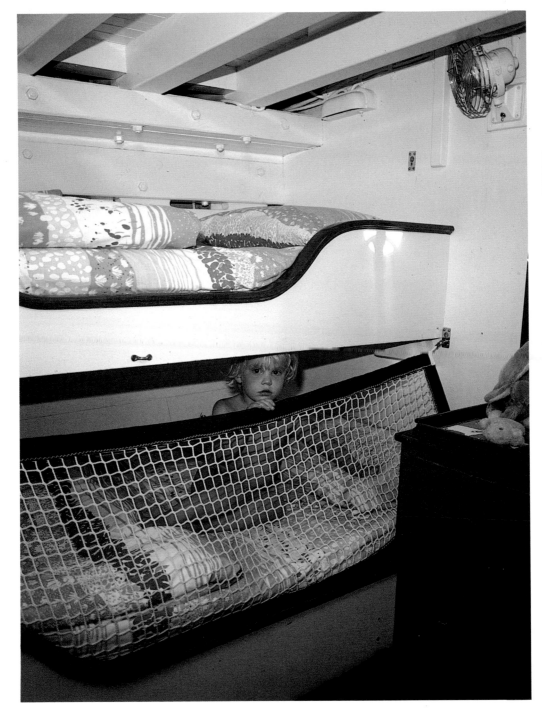

DELIVERANCE

U ntil 1935 *Edna*, a Dutch Luger, was a drift net fishing boat searching out herring in the North Sea. From 1935-1973, she hauled cargo in the Baltic. She was laid up in Denmark from 1973 until 1978, when Brad Ives, a determined young man from Maine, returned her to the cargo trade.

Brad began the renovations in Aalborg, Denmark, replating some of the topsides, changing the fo'c'sle accommodations, and purchasing essential new gear. *Edna* was subsequently taken to Leixoes, Portugal, where rebuilding began in earnest. With a new mast, spars, deck, deck house, and a freshly chipped and painted underdeck, *Edna* set out on a shakedown cruise in April, 1980 to the Canary Islands, West Indies, Boston, and Maine.

The crew of the *Edna* includes Brad's seafaring wife, Linda, who has skippered boats of her own, and their children, Simon, eight, and Willow, four, and from two to six crew.

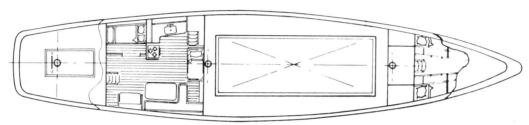

The main living area aft of the cargo hold consists of Brad and Linda's private cabin, the galley, and a dining area, most of which was constructed out of dunnage gathered from throughout the boat. The large dining table, for example, was the previous galley door.

An athwartship bunk for young Willow and her dolls dominates the forward bulkhead of this rustic, but homey, main saloon. Jordan, Dana's baby, agreed to pose for us along with the ship's new puppy, since Willow was not available at the moment. A nice touch to the main saloon is the herb garden under the skylight.

Type:	Topsail Ketch
LOA:	130'
LOD:	100'
Beam:	21'6"
Depth of hold:	10'
Draft:	10' light
Cargo capacity:	150 tons, 6500 cu. ft.
Engine:	B&W Alpha Diesel, 200 b.h.p.
Rig:	Topsail Ketch
Generator:	Lister Diesel, 12kw 440v, 3 2kw 24v
Builder:	J. Figgee Co. in Vlardingen, Holland
Year:	1916, rebuilt in 1979
Hull:	Riveted steel construction

Simon and the rest of the crew live in the quarters forward of the cargo hold, which has two small double cabins and four communal uppers and lowers. Everybody has use of the head, which occupies a quiet private space on the afterdeck.

The engine room is magnificently maintained with a frequent fresh coat of fire engine red paint. *Edna* carries a full workshop, air compressor, oxy-acetylene gear, and an electric welder.

Brad and Linda are devoted to the live-aboard cargo business. *Edna* is not just their boat, but a way of life. Their children receive the Calvert School Correspondence course and usually one of the crew assists Linda in daily tutoring.

In 1981 *Edna* took a load of blue jeans and T shirts to West Africa and returned to the West Indies with timber, baskets and cloth. In New England they picked up construction materials to take to the West Indies. Well, it's one way of seeing the world. After all in 1982 *Edna* plans to sail to the South Pacific.

ENCHANTA

We were initially drawn to "Enchanta" because of her long sleek lines. We found her interior matches the elegance of her exterior.

Originally commissioned in 1953, *Enchanta* had a total refit in 1978. The owners, Dr. and Mrs. Norman Traverse, of Lexington, Massachusetts are proud of their personal touches. Employed as a luxury charter boat in New England and the Caribbean, *Enchanta* is maintained by a professional crew.

The aft cabin is paneled in solid American walnut. This stateroom contains an extra large double bunk, bureau vanity, stereo, bronze fireplace, and the biggest surprise of all, a built in armchair. Further accentuating a touch of class, is the extensive library and original oil paintings. The bookshelves are well crafted with fiddles designed to keep the books securely in place. The armchair looks more suited to a townhouse than a sailing yacht, but in fact we think it's a practical addition. Reading is one of the favorite pastimes on so many boats, and slouching for a long period of time in a bunk can be excruciating to the tailbone. Another nice effect in the aft cabin are the opening skylights. One of them is directly over the bed, offering a romantic view of the sky.

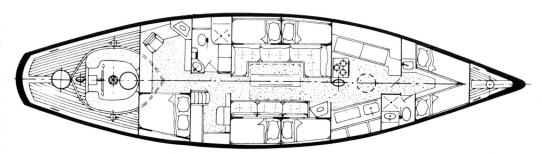

Type:	Yawl
LOA:	67'
LWL:	51'
Beam:	15' 7"
Sail Area:	2,630 sq. ft.
Displacement:	68 tons
Hull Construction:	steel (1" thick at keel)
Engine:	GM 4-71
Commissioned:	1953
Complete Refit:	1978
Naval Architect:	John G. Alden Company
Builder:	Abeking & Rasmussen, Germany
Interior Designer:	Phyllis Feld of Boston

The main saloon, head, and navigation area are finished in a natural teak. The word natural is so popular today and evokes a certain earthy image, but the raw teak used here has a bleached out appearance and does not emit the same warmth as the walnut in the aft cabin. The whole saloon is rather stark and formal. The two focal points are the highly polished bronze dropleaf table and bronze fireplace. Both are dramatically beautiful. The high sheen polished effect is decorative and impressive. It is also quite susceptible to fingerprints and smudges. It's a good thing *Enchanta* has a full time paid crew aboard.

The galley is forward of the main saloon, which is not our favorite location for a galley. We'll make a concession to John Alden this time, because it is

well ventilated and functional. There is a stainless steel sink and work area designed for ease of cleaning. There are well placed cupboards for easy access to dishes and cooking utensils. Wooden pegs keep the pewter plates separated and secure. The most exciting feature of the galley is the large, freestanding butcher block in the center of the galley floor. It has a built-in pull-out, ventilated vegetable bin. It provides a great place to cut, chop and peel, away from the cracks and crevices of the (toploading) icebox. The cook can also use the block to lean against in a seaway.

The navigator's station has all the latest electronic devices and equipment, including a Kelvin-Hughes 24-mile radar, Micro instruments, computerized Loran C, and even an intercom system.

ESCAPADE

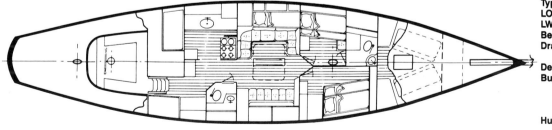

Type:	Yawl
LOA:	73'
LWL:	53'
Beam:	17'
Draft: CBU:	7'6"
CBD:	13'
Designer:	Philip L. Rhodes
Builder:	Luders Marine Construction Co. of Stamford, Connecticut
Hull:	Philippine mahogany on white oak frames
Deck:	Burma teak. all fastenings and diagonal strapping of bronze
Year:	1938

Escapade! She is as provocative as her name suggests. This magnificent 73' wooden Yawl is world famous. Her sleek lines and raked masts are recognizable in any harbor.

Designed by Philip Rhodes and built by Luders in Stamford, Connecticut, *Escapade* made her racing debut in the 1938 Bermuda Race. Having been campaigned as a racing boat until recent years, *Escapade* maintains the present day distinction of still holding several world records. Lately, *Escapade* has participated in select races such as the Nantucket Opera House Cup Race, the Newport Classic Boat Regatta, and the "down island" annuals, such as the St. Barts Regatta and Antigua Sailing Week—all the fun ones!

In addition to her outstanding sailing performance, *Escapade* offers the ultimate in luxurious cruising. Below decks, forward of the galley and navigation area, is a spacious main saloon (7'3" headroom). The main cabin is paneled in both teak and mahogany. On the port side is an L shaped settee. Behind the settee is an alcove-like pilot berth. Numerous velvet pillows make this area a cozy nook to nestle in. The mahogany dining table seats at least eight comfortably. On the starboard side is another settee. The wine-colored velour upholstery and the Persian rug enhance the interior with an Old World charm.

Forward of the main saloon are two private double cabins. Crew quarters are in the fo' c'sle. There are two heads (fore and aft) with hot and cold pressure water and a shower.

The aft galley is well ventilated and designed with a convenient "pass-through" to the pilothouse and cockpit. *Escapade* has a large cockpit table for on-deck dining.

Photograph by Gil Frei

Photograph by Gil Frei

EYOLA

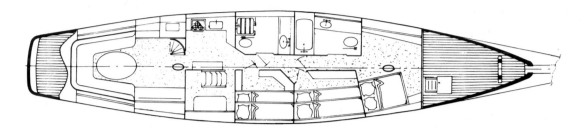

Type:	Brigantine Schooner
LOA:	90'
LOD:	75'
Beam:	17'
Draft:	8'6"
Displacement:	79 tons
Sail Area:	2,780 sq. ft.
Builder/ Place:	Owners, Hennie and Eugene Page, Durbin, South Africa
Designer:	Peter Strong
Year:	Completed 1977
Hull:	Ferro cement
Engine:	Caterpillar Diesel

Photograph by Hennie Page

Eyola is a unique Brigantine Schooner. We're not sure which has more character, the interior, or the owners, Hennie and Eugene Page. The Pages are an enthusiastic couple who charter *Eyola* out of St. Thomas, U.S. Virgin Islands.

They built the boat themselves and take a lot of pride in its eccentricities. The aft main saloon is paneled in teak, salvaged from an old South African Railroad carriage. Other woods used in the boat were gathered from various old buildings such as a former girl's school. Thus *Eyola* has incorporated into her interior structure assorted roof beams and floorboards from around South Africa.

You enter the aft saloon by descending a spiral staircase. There is a large oblong teak dining table with a wraparound brown velour settee. Glass paneled teak cupboards hold the antique crystal, porcelain and silver.

The galley, cabins, heads and navigation area are all forward of the main saloon and have a separate on deck entrance hatch. The galley is done in yellow and black Japanese tile. There are louvered slats on the cupboards for ventilation. The Pages use an American Hardwick stove and stow the propane tanks on deck. Forward of the galley, also on the port side, is a head with a lavatory and stall shower. Opposite the companionway on the starboard side are two private guest cabins head to foot each with its own vanity and sink. Forward from beam to beam is a super large master stateroom with a head, bathtub, sink and vanity *en suite*, the bulkhead of which backs onto the communal head. Convenient for the plumber, and luxurious for the lucky guests who win this cabin. The heads are finished in Italian tile. In the master stateroom, with its freestanding double bed, leather chair, bathtub and domestic flushing toilet, you might forget you are on a boat. The other heads are seafaring LaVac toilets. The cabins are paneled in English oak, and the heads are decorated with Italian tile.

For those who are bored with boats that look like boats, *Eyola* is a whimsical example of a nonconventional nautical interior.

FIREBIRD

*F*irebird circumnavigated the world before settling into the charter trade. Sparkling white, eternally clean and new looking, *Firebird*'s interior is refreshing. There is a modern multi level concept inherent in her design. The navigation area and crew's quarters are one level below the cockpit; then the main saloon is a step down again. The saloon, with its generous settee and table, is bright and airy. The galley is a practical U-shape, with a dining area conveniently adjacent to it.

There is a guest cabin to port of the main saloon that has two single berths and its own head and shower, and another cabin and head forward of the galley that has two uppers and lowers.

Most spacious is the master stateroom aft of the center cockpit. This cabin has a large double berth, a single berth *and* its own private cockpit. This small aft cockpit doubles as a Jacuzzi hot tub. Simply stopper it and fill with water—voilá!

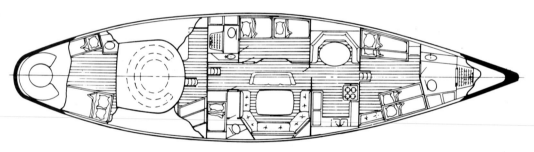

Type:	Motor Sailer Ketch
LOA:	85'
LOD:	84'
Beam:	18'
Draft:	10'
Builder:	Palmer & Johnson, Sturgeon Bay, Wisconsin
Designer:	Sparkman & Stephens
Year:	1968
Hull:	Aluminum

Photographs by Collin Robson

FISH HAWK

Photograph by Jeffrey Barrows

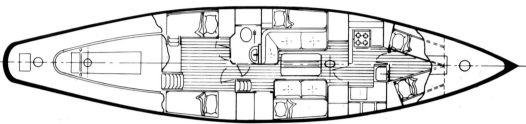

Type:	Cutter
Length:	62'9"
Beam:	14'9"
Draft:	8'
Builder:	Gaudy & Stevens, East Boothbay, Maine
Designer:	John G. Alden
Year:	1937
Hull:	Double planked mahogany over oak Teak decks
Engine:	Mercedes Diesel, 4-cyl, 85 h.p.

Fish Hawk is one of those perfect specimens of vintage Aldens that wooden boat lovers gravitate towards. She is sleek and sweet.

Originally commissioned by a prominent U.S. Senator and former Massachusetts governor, *Fish Hawk* was owned by the same family for 37 years. During that time she was maintained in mint condition by a professional captain. The present owner, Jeffrey Barrows of Middleton, Massachusetts, has certainly preserved the tradition that is *Fish Hawk's* birthright.

1980 marked *Fish Hawk's* first experience as a charter boat in the Virgin Islands. The interior has that graceful color combination of bright white paint accented by rich mahogany trim. There is nothing gloomy about this wooden boat. The settees in the main saloon have been newly upholstered with a coral and seaweed plaid pattern, adding a modern compliment to the leaded glass cabinets and solid brass oil lamps. Nooks and crannies behind the settees are perfect catchall places.

The galley is quite efficient, with special slots for cups and glasses. It has been renovated to include an Adler-Barbour refrigerator and shipmate propane stove. The tanks are stowed on deck aft of the fo'c'sle hatch. One of the nicest places on board is the aft cabin. There is a double bunk with a short settee in front of it and a built-in dresser and hanging locker. The large overhead hatch lets in a lot of light and air.

The cabin sole is fabricated of cork. Before making her debut in the Caribbean, *Fish Hawk* spent a lot of time at Dions Yard in Salem, Massachusetts. Barrows particularly recommends them for restoring old boats.

FREEDOM

Freedom, skippered by Dennis Conner, was the 1980 winner of the legendary Americas Cup Race. She defended the title against France, Sweden, Great Britain and Australia. The Americas Cup is the longest held trophy in the history of sport: 123 years.

The term 12 Meter refers to the end product of a mathematical formula that relates a set number of boats dimensions; i.e. length plus two times her girth difference minus her freeboard plus the square root of her sail area divided by 2.37 must equal twelve:

$$\frac{L + 2d - F + \sqrt{S}}{2.37} = 12$$

Freedom is owned by Maritime College at Ft. Shuyler Foundation. We went aboard her after one of the preliminary trials at her berth at Williams and Manchester in Newport, Rhode Island. She is a mean machine, not exactly fitted out for leisurely cruising. The Americas Cup Race these days is one of high technology. After having been aboard *Gleam*, the old 12 meter built in 1937, the difference in interior design is striking.

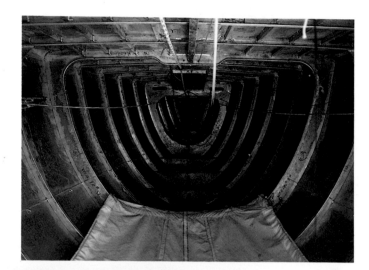

Type:	Sloop
LOA:	63′
LWL:	47′
Draft:	9′
Beam:	12′ 5″
Built:	Minnefords, New York
Designer:	Sparkman & Stephens
Hull:	Aluminum

Photograph by Dan Nerney

GALIA

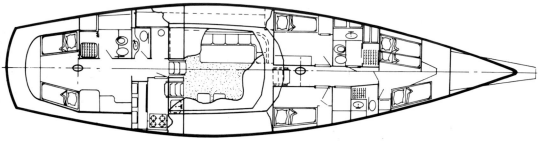

Type:	Bermuda ketch
LOA:	80'
Beam:	19'
Draft:	10'6"
Builder:	Yates, S.A., in Argentina
Designer:	Roberto Rovere
Hull:	Diagonally planked mahogany on oak, with a thin layer of fiberglass over it
Launched:	1979

Galia is an ultra modern, very sexy sailing yacht owned by David Azrieli of Montreal. The main cabin enjoys a panoramic view of the outside world. The vast wraparound windows are made of smoked bulletproof glass. They slide open for fresh air, yet, when closed, they are immensely strong. The cabin walls are dramatically finished in black Formica. The main saloon couch is upholstered in deep brown leather, and the cabin sole is carpeted in a handsome taupe wool. The dining table in front of the curved couch is constructed of maple root, as is the freestanding bar to starboard in the main saloon. The table is constructed so that it can pull out and expand to seat a large dinner party. Behind the bar are built-in drawers with customized slots for the dishes and cutlery.

The aft cabin has the aura of a swank bachelor pad. There is a window built into the transom behind the king-size bed. The bulkheads are upholstered in tan leather. In front of the bed is a parlor area with a coffee-colored suede couch and charcoal brown wool carpeting. The master head has a stainless steel bathtub, stainless steel sink on a granite counter top with inlaid marble faucet taps and a bidet.

The navigation room, located between the master stateroom and the main saloon, is completely self contained and very practical. There is a proper size chart table, large enough to spread charts out such that no folding is necessary. Underneath the table is a fitted bin designed to accommodate the largest unfolded chart. The navigator's stool pivots on a pedestal. The navigation area has all B&G instruments, SSB radio and an intercom system extending to the foredeck crew and the helmsman.

The electric panel is a work of art, color coded and reminiscent of a flight engineer's panel in an airliner. The skipper was proud of all of the innovations on board, from the stainless steel superstructure of the bilge, to novel ideas on deck. For instance, at the bow of the boat there is a grating over the anchor designed to protect your feet when doing any bowsprit work. Yet it is readily removable when you need to get at the anchor. Other design features are the recessed anchor windlass, large sliding hatch for easy below deck stowage of jibs, and an on-deck shower. Two guest cabins are located forward of the main saloon. All cabins and heads have stereo and intercom system.

The crew's quarters forward are fully self contained with a private on-deck entrance.

The galley is forward and to starboard of the main saloon. It is efficiently laid out in all black Formica and stainless steel. The effect is striking, but a trifle gloomy.

There are plenty of amusements on board: video equipment, Betamax, Atari TV games, and a movie camera.

Galia is one of the most unusual boats we have seen and demonstrates a proper use of modern materials in an honest manner. No wood grained Formica or simulated planking here.

GALIA

GLEAM

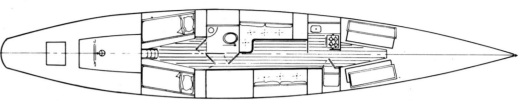

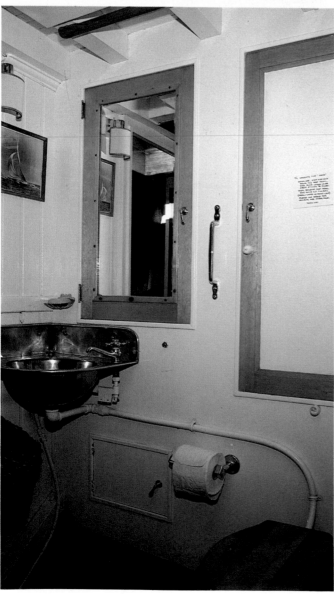

G*leam* was designed by Clinton Crane for his own personal use. She has always been owned by past commodores of the Sewanaka Corinthian and New York Yacht Clubs.

Gleam is presently owned by a young Newport, Rhode Island couple, Bob and Lisa Tiedeman. They race her, cruise her, sometimes charter her, but mostly enjoy her. *Gleam* represents a special tradition of 12 meter yachts. Built prior to WWII, before the rules for racing were altered, *Gleam* is the last 12 meter that was designed with a cruising interior. Post *Gleam*, racing vessels became less and less suitable for civilized cruising. The original interior is beautifully handcrafted out of an assortment of woods. The main saloon is paneled in western red cedar. There are four berths (two folding berths), dining table, and leaded glass cabinets. A large skylight overhead adds light and air to the main cabin.

The forward galley, recently renovated by the Tiedemans, incorporates two kinds of woods: Albino mahogany, and a lightweight wood called obeche. Currently it boasts a large refrigerator/freezer, a Shipmate stove, and an overhead hatch—altogether a fine culinary environment.

The aft cabin has two large berths with settees, plenty of drawers, two hanging lockers, and bookshelves above the bunks. One of the hanging lockers has a rack that pulls out athwartships to make it easier to hang clothes and is kept in place by a pin.

The common head is a real classic. It is large, because at the time the 12 meter specifications required it. A shiny copper sink and a natural maple toilet seat are distinctive.

We encountered *Gleam* at the 1980 Classic Boat Race in Newport, where she was the overall winner of the race. She is seen here with the *Pride of Baltimore*.

Type:	Sloop
LOA:	67'11"
LWL:	46'11"
Beam:	12'
Draft:	8'10"
Builder:	Henry B. Nevins, City Island, New York
Designer:	Clinton Crane
Year:	1937
Hull:	Double-planked mahogany on cedar skin on oak frames

ISLA DE IBIZA

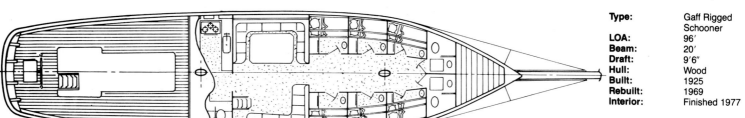

Type:	Gaff Rigged Schooner
LOA:	96'
Beam:	20'
Draft:	9'6"
Hull:	Wood
Built:	1925
Rebuilt:	1969
Interior:	Finished 1977

Isla de Ibiza is owned and operated as a charter vessel in the Virgin Islands by a delightful couple, Tio and Ursula Breider. Years ago the boat was a Spanish fishing schooner. The Brieders spent a lot of time and care making Isla special.

The main cabin is very woodsy and homey. There is plenty of space on board for twelve charter guests in six private double cabins with four heads and three showers. Each cabin is bright and cheerfully decorated. Ursula made custom sheets, bedspreads and towels for all of the cabins. There are two heads with showers forward of the cabins.

The galley is spacious, with a convenient pass-through to the main saloon. The whole boat is an example of creativity and ingenuity. For example, Tio fluted the hatch coaming in order to hide the scars from her fishing days.

Although being put to an entirely new and different use, the overall impression is one of harmony with her past.

JANETTE

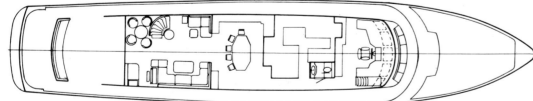

Type: Motor Yacht
Length: 117′6″
Beam: 25′2″
Draft: 6′7″ full load
6′4″ half load
LOA: 118′5″
Gross tonnage: 170
Net tonnage: 136
Power: Twin Mercedes MTU, 1,350 HP each
Builder: Rochester, England
Designer: William Williamson/ Profiles: Jon Bannenberg
Construction: Aluminum
Year: Completed 1978

Janette is a modern flying bridge motor yacht with cockpit. For the last couple of years she has been wintering in Florida and the Bahamas and summering in Long Island Sound and New England. Available for worldwide charter, *Janette* carries 11,750 gallons of fuel and cruises at about 18 knots.

Well designed for entertaining, she has ample space to lounge around from the foredeck to the quarterdeck sunlounge. The two large cushioned couches on the foredeck double as storage deck boxes. The wheelhouse is well equipped with electronic devices to aid in navigation. There is a chart table and observation couch at the rear of the wheelhouse beyond the helmsman seat. Bookcases, storage shelf, foul-weather gear closet and large storage closet are below the wheelhouse deck. Next is the guest deck off the starboard passage. There is a pressure head and mirrored cabinet. The Sherle Wagner sink is an elaborate shell-shaped onyx sculpture. With gold plated fittings, this sink is one of the most handsome features of *Janette*'s interior.

The galley is completely electric and is equipped to serve banquets of any size, with two ovens, two broilers, a rotisserie, walk-in freezer, large refrigerator, garbage disposal, trash compactor, D/W, electric charcoal grill, pantry and more.

The dining salon has an unusual metal sculptured table for ten, with extension leaves to accommodate 14 people. On the port side is a full-width credenza for linen storage while athwartship there is a specially designed carved bleached rosewood breakfront to hold the crystal, dishes and sterling in fitted cushioned cabinetry. Between the main saloon and the dining area is an archway with a brass grilled folding door. This archway and dividing bulkhead is also fabricated out of bleached rosewood. The saloon is fully carpeted and arranged like any proper living room with couches, love seats, swivel chairs, club chair grouping, bridge table and chairs, wetbar, and, of course, a sparkling white baby grand piano.

A 12 foot window wall aft of the saloon opens to the sundeck. In case you would rather watch TV outside instead of in, here is the place to do it. The aft deck has a curved couch, high/low dining table for eight to ten people. From here is a spiral stair to the boat deck and two stairways aft to the fishing cockpit.

The fishing cockpit has two full size Pompanette "barber" fishing chairs, cabinet for fishing tackle, gear and rods. There is a flush-deck capstan, storage cabinet for Tide Ride ladders, all weather intercom station, salt and fresh water outlets. Also for the lucky fisherman is a live bait well and fish box. You don't even have to go below to freshen up after the fight. There is a hot and cold shower to accommodate the fishermen and the swimmers.

The below deck accommodations are suitable for nine in the owners party, with five heads: two in the master stateroom and one apiece in each of the guest cabins. The master stateroom is paneled in bleached beechwood.

JENS JUHL

The *Jens Juhl* was built in Denmark in 1940 and run as a cargo boat in the North Sea. During the war she performed the heroic deed of running refugees from occupied countries to Sweden. At one point a bridge collapsed on the boat, reducing her rigging to one steadying mast and sail.

In the last twelve years, the "Juhl" has had two owners, Kenneth Mitchnick, and John Summers. She has crisscrossed the Atlantic a few times but has spent the majority of time trading cargo in the West Indies. The Trinidadians hailed her as the cargo yacht because the bright work and brass were always gleaming. Even the engine room was sparkling white.

Until she was sold in 1981 the whole cargo operation was run as a communal enterprise with profits going back into the boat and to the general happy life style aboard.

Since much of this boat's space is taken up by the cargo hold, the actual living quarters are confined to a forepeak cabin and an aft main cabin entered through the pilothouse.

The fo'c'sle with its private entrance forward of the cargo hold is quite spacious accommodating two double bunks. The white bulkheads and deck prisms contribute a bright airy feeling. This cabin is a favorite among the *Jens Juhl* crew because it affords quietude and privacy.

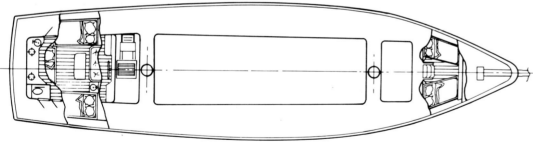

Type:	Baltic Trader
LOA:	120'
LOD:	90'
Beam:	24'
Draft:	10'6" loaded; 8'6" empty
Builder:	Nykobing Mors, Denmark
Year:	1940
Rerigged:	1979—Hobro, Denmark
Engine:	B&W Alpha

The main saloon, with its exposed beams and timbers, reminds one of a log cabin. Three oversize double bunks surround the area, except for the forward bulkhead which has a settee and mahogany dining table. There is also an unusual wooden wash basin fabricated of a large Haitian bowl with a lovely brass faucet. The bunks are cozily endowed with big and small pillows colorfully covered in a medley of java prints and Caribbean fabrics.

There is a library and stereo system extending almost the entire length of the aft bulkhead behind the captain's bunk. Wicker baskets abound and wooden Dewars Scotch boxes with rope handles are used as drawers. They fit nicely below the bunks. The portholes are small, but there is a significant opening skylight above the dining table.

The wheelhouse is both functional and beautiful. It's a protected environment for the helmsman, navigator, and a peaceful retreat for the cook after preparing a meal for the masses.

The galley backs onto the wheelhouse. It's wonderful to have an "on deck" galley; there's never a problem with claustrophobia or lack of ventilation. The cook has a picture window above the counter and sink and full-length open doors, both port and starboard. The forward bulkhead adjacent to the wheelhouse is taken up with a rectangular icebox 4' x 1½', incorporating a pine cutting board.

The galley counter is a lovely handcrafted piece of African hardwood called kungalo. There is a small propane oven and two single propane burners. One of the stoves, a Neptune, made in Denmark, features a ring with three levers that clamp into place, adjusting to various pot sizes.

Because *Jens Juhl* is a work boat, most of the plates and cups are wooden or sturdy plastic. Dishes are stowed under the sink on a shelf with a drain to the deck. Knives, forks, spoons and other cooking utensils are stowed country kitchen style, upright in bamboo cups. The galley serves well the prodigious food requirements aboard the *Juhl*.

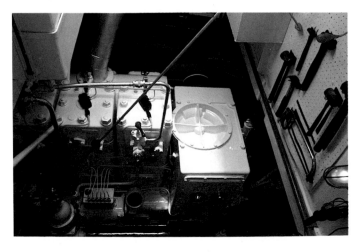

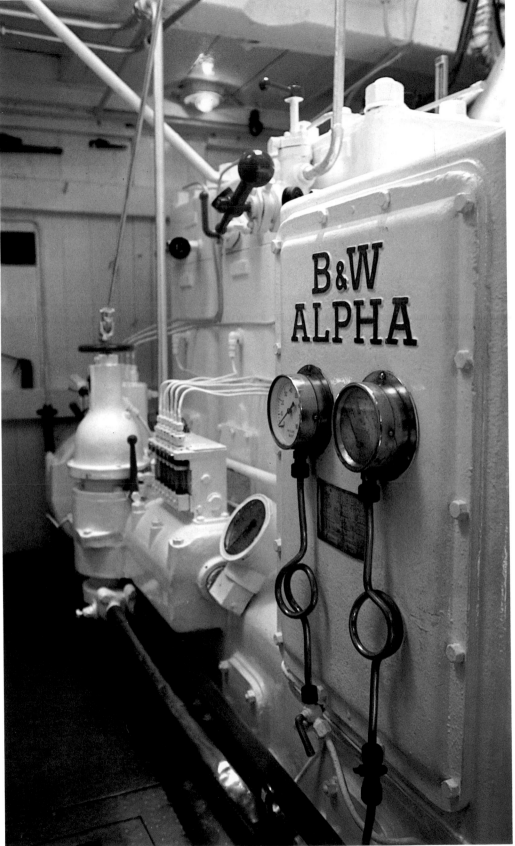

JENS JUHL

KIALOA III

Type:	Sloop
Length:	79′
Beam:	11′4″
Draft:	11′6″
Builder:	Palmer Johnson, Sturgeon Bay, Wisconsin
Designer:	Sparkman & Stephens, modified by David Pedrick
Sail Area:	2,733 sq. ft.
Hull Construction:	Aluminum

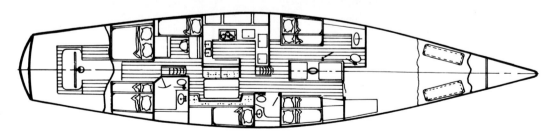

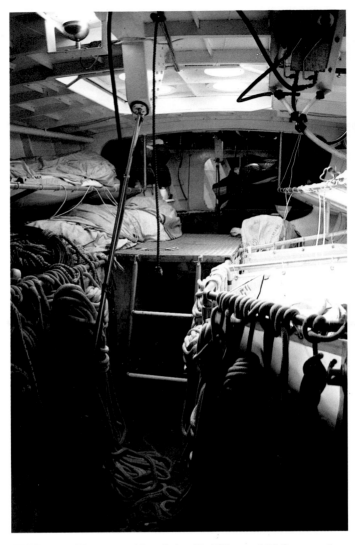

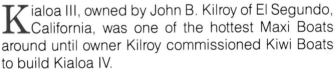

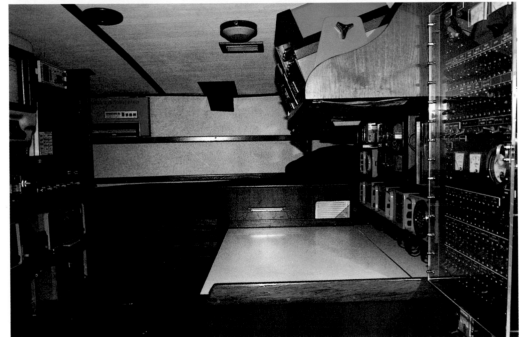

Kialoa III, owned by John B. Kilroy of El Segundo, California, was one of the hottest Maxi Boats around until owner Kilroy commissioned Kiwi Boats to build Kialoa IV.

Extremely competitive in 'round the world races, Kialoa is surprisingly well fitted out for cruising. Paneled in teak is a luxurious aft cabin and pleasant dining area in the main saloon.

The galley is formed in a large square, with an athwartships Grunert refrigerator/freezer at one end. The refrigerator is designed with a canned drink or beer dispenser at the bottom. A long fore and aft sea swing, rigged with stainless steel stanchions, supports a general purpose counter. The skipper says it seemed like a good idea at the time, but was not that effective as a gimbaling system.

The navigation station, so important for racing tactics, is extemely tidy and well appointed. In fact the whole boat is laid out for efficiency. For instance, in addition to hooks at the foot of the companionway, there is a wet locker with its own heater for quick drying and a separate locker for sea boots. The sail stowage area, as one would expect, is enormous to acccmmodate all of the racing sails.

LENE MARIE

Lene Marie hauled cargo until the 1960s. In 1970-71 she was converted into a pleasure craft and has undergone continual renovation since. She is currently owned by the Sausalito Waterfront Company. Three principals in the company, Peter Stocker, Bill Harlan, and John Montgomery, bought her in 1975, trading seven building sites near Lake Tahoe for her.

Lene Marie is quite impressive on deck. Her rigging is incredibly massive. The main saloon is similarly memorable, rustic in the way of a log cabin and about that size. The interior woods are fir, mahogany, and the dining table is rosewood. The galley has a commercial refrigerator/freezer and a stainless steel diesel stove. The fir counters have been polyurethane protected. Part of the galley enclosure acts as a bar.

The main saloon is randomly arranged with director chairs, wicker chairs covered in java print fabric and strawmats. Four pilot berths have privacy curtains and contribute to the ambiance of the cabin. Forward of the main saloon are four additional bunks. The two private staterooms aft are roomy, as you would expect.

The navigation station is in the main saloon near the dining area, complete with ham radio, radar and VHF radio. Above the chart table is complete fishing gear stowage.

Lene Marie, without denying her heritage, has become a classic, if not classy, yacht.

Type:	Baltic Trader
LOA:	106'
Beam:	20'
Draft:	7½'
Displacement:	100 tons
Builder:	Otto Hansen, Stubbekobing, Denmark
Year:	1910
Hull:	Oak on oak
Engine:	GM Diesel

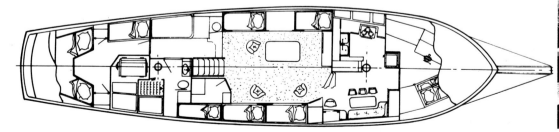

LINDØ

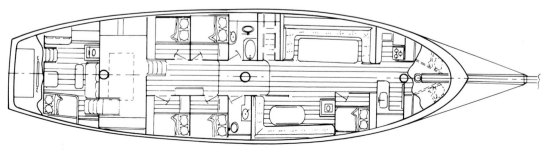

Type:	Baltic Trader
LOA:	125'
LOD:	92'
Beam:	22'
Gross Tons:	102
Builder:	Albert Svansson, Blekinge, Sweden
Designer:	Karl Ogard
Year:	1927
Hull:	Pitch pine on oak below the water line, oak on oak above the water line
Total sail area:	7,000 sq. ft.
Engine:	Mercedes diesel, 185 hp

With her black hull, red sails and three ten-story high masts, *Lindø* looks like a true pirate ship. In fact, when Peter Benchley's book, *The Island* was made into a movie, *Lindø* was hired for exactly that role. Famous not only for her looks, *Lindø* placed third overall in the 1976 Op Sail Tall Ships race. In 1980, with a crew of sailing students, she also placed second in the U.S.-to-Norway leg of the 1980 Tall Ships Series.

Lindø is Danish for "island of the Lindou trees." Many Baltic Traders have been built in Scandinavia, but *Lindø* is probably one of the finest in existence. Sturdy and heavily built, she hauled cargo years ago: iron, salt and timber from Scandinavia to Nova Scotia and the West Indies. Today she is a charter vessel renovated to impeccable yacht standards.

The enormous main saloon includes a large dining table and separate lounging area. It's a delight to have enough room aboard a sailing vessel to allow for a special area to relax or read in. There is a pleasant semi-circular couch, coffee table and library opposite a beautiful polished brass fireplace just for this purpose. The galley is just forward of and facing the dining area. Extending beam to beam there is plenty of working and stowage space. The counters are German maple butcher block. The refrigerator is a cold plate system that runs off the Lister generator. There is access to the back of the freezer (the whole unit lifts out) to make it convenient to check for rot or any mechanical problem that might arise. Meals for 17 are not uncommon aboard *Lindø*.

There are five double cabins, each cozy with exposed wooden beams, colorful bedspreads and oil lamps. The ship's heads have beautiful wooden counters with red sinks and gold plated faucets. One of the heads has a matching red bathtub.

A passage aft leads to the engine room and a well organized workshop.

The aft captain's cabin is luxurious with its own fireplace, velvet settee, antique desk, brass lamps and double bunk. The navigation station occupies a portion of this generous cabin. *Lindø* is such a large vessel—carrying six or seven crew and ten charter guests—that such luxurious accommodations for the skipper are not only a privilege, but a necessity.

NIRVANA

Intended as a hot racer, *Nirvana* was commissioned just six days prior to the 1950 Bermuda race. She was in the lead when the wind picked up, but having no reef points, she was forced to drop her mainsail. She still managed to come in third. Subsequently, she was sold to Nelson Rockefeller, remaining his private yacht until recent years when she was purchased by David Ray of Bannisters Wharf in Newport, Rhode Island.

A classic beauty, she is the largest wooden boat Hinckley ever built. A proper yacht in every sense of the word, her interior is immaculately well groomed, with nothing out of place. The main saloon, painted white with mahogany trim, is dressed in deep shades of navy blue with corduroy upholstery on the settees and pilot berths. The mahogany table is varnished to a bright finish and the polished brass fireplace further enhances the touch of class.

The galley is efficient for both charter catering and cooking on passage. With this particular galley layout, it was advantageous to mount the stove athwartships. A universal joint attached from behind enables the stove to maintain a full gimbaled effect. There is ample space for food preparation, yet the galley is compact enough to give the cook security in a seaway. A cabinet over the sink cleverly allows wet dishes to be stored vertically and drain into it. A deep freezer under the cabin sole is used primarily for extra provisions during passages.

Nirvana, a Buddhist term exemplifying the ultimate freedom from pain, worry, and the external world, is a befitting name.

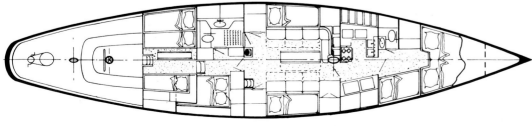

Type:	Yawl
LOA:	65'
LWL:	45'
Beam:	14'3"
Draft:	8'4"
Displacement:	35 tons
Designer:	John G. Alden
Built:	Hinckley's Yard, Maine
Year completed:	1950; Refit: 1979
Hull:	Mahogany on oak, double planked cedar
Engine:	G.M. Diesel

NOW VOYAGER

Type:	Motor Yacht
Length:	68'6"
Beam:	16'4"
Draft:	5'6"
Displacement:	51 tons
Builder:	Quincy Adams Boatyard, Quincy, Massachusetts
Designer:	Dermit McGuinness
Year:	1956
Hull:	Double planked mahogany
Engine:	Twin GM6-71 diesels

Now Voyager is a classic Down East Motor Yacht, handcrafted by New England artisans. The main saloon has a friendliness so often lacking in powerboats that is derived from a proper combination of white paint, mahogany trim and yellow knotty pine. Recently, the wicker chairs and couch were reupholstered in bright Marimekko fabrics. The dining alcove and cabin bedspreads are also alive with this cheery all cotton material.

Now Voyager is a charterboat in the Virgin Islands. Her skipper is Robert Befeld and the cook is Robyne Holt from Australia. Robyne finds her galley spacious, light and well-designed to work in. There are two stoves: propane and an electric Corning Ware stovetop. Also there is a Grunert refrigerator/freezer cold plate system. At dockside they can plug into shore power; or, at anchor, they must run their 15-kw Kohler generator for their A/C and other electrical appliances, such as the Mr. Coffee you see on the galley counter. There are hooks for cups, special slots for dishes and a fixed spice rack. Cannisters are within reach on the ledge behind the dining alcove. Robyne puts double-sided tape on the bottom to keep them from sliding, and she places felt on the bottom of her plants to slow their slide. Last year Robyne authored a cookbook, From Galleys for Guests, in conjunction with some other charterboat cooks.

Belowdeck level, the crew's quarters are forward, and there are three double guest cabins with two full baths. The cabins are painted white with mahogany trim. The aft stateroom has private stairs leading to the aft cockpit.

The captain's bridge is a delightful spot with its large mahogany helm and panoramic view.

Now Voyager is certainly a comfortable way to go cruising!

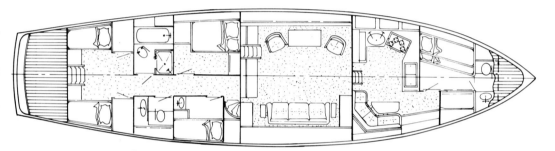

ONDINE

Type:	Ketch
Length:	79'
Beam:	17'4"
Displacement:	81,950 lb.
Built:	Derektor's Yard, Mamaroneck, New York
Year:	1974
Designed by:	Briton Chance
Redesigned by:	Jerry Milgram—1976
Hull:	Aluminum

Ondine is a maxi-boat. Whenever her name is mentioned, someone has always just seen her in the Med, at Block Island or Bermuda.

Her baby blue deck exhibits a wealth of impressive racing gear. Sumner "Huey" Long has owned a number of Ondines striving for the ultimate racing machine. Not satisfied with this Ondine, he commissioned Jerry Milgram to institute some alterations.

The Milgram redesign contributes significant changes in rig and underbody. In particular, she was converted from a sloop to ketch and the centerboard was removed.

Her main saloon, since the change, appears to have been influenced by modern abstract sculpture. Interesting, and not entirely unpleasant, are these white painted stress members. The centerboard case has made a smooth transition to liquor locker and safe. The Derektor-designed, articulated and gimbaled table, accommodates dinner for 18.

The navigation station has all of the tricks of the trade, necessary to plot a winning course.

The galley too, keeping in mind the racing crew, is large and functional. The counter space has easy-to-clean stainless fiddles and an enormous pit for pot and pan stowage. The cook advocates tall pots to reduce spillage. Ample food storage and a 20 cu. ft. freezer beneath the galley sole allow the cook to plan well in advance. Sleeping accommodations are abundant, with scores of upper and lower bunks in the main saloon and after section. Privacy is lacking, but then racing is a sport of cameraderie. (Bringing up the rear of the boat; a sauna, of course).

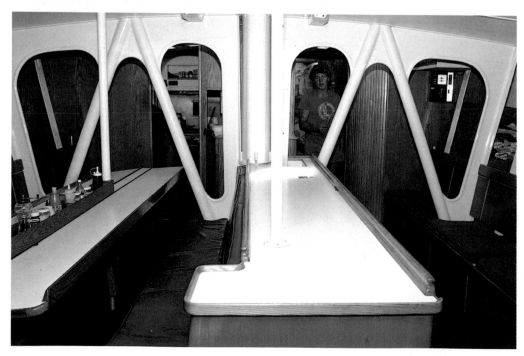

PALAWAN

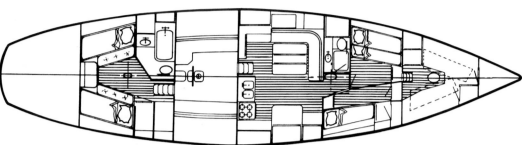

Type:	Ketch
LOA:	67'6"
Beam:	17'6"
Draft:	6'8"
Builder:	Abeking & Rasmussen, Germany
Designer:	Sparkman & Stephens
Year:	1972
Hull:	Aluminum

Palawan traveled 60,000 miles during a period of seven years. She is as clean as a whistle. When the former captain Paul Wolters gave us the grand tour in Camden, Maine, she looked ready to set forth on another long voyage. However, *Palawan* had been sold by owner, Tom Watson, to a group called Caribbean/New England Charters. Even though the boat was in transitional ownership when we photographed her, it was apparent that she was always kept in immaculate condition. Even her engine room beneath the cockpit sole, is beautiful and well organized.

The interior is paneled in teak, ordinary fare for a boat. However, this boat is highly unusual in that the teak is all from one tree. Therefore, the paneling is all solid wood and perfectly matched.

As you descend the stairs to the main saloon, there is a tidy L shaped galley to port and a no nonsense navigation station to starboard. The galley has a double stainless steel sink with both pressure water and a hand pump. The counters are flush so that a sponge can sweep directly from the counter into the sink. Similarly, the top loading refrigerator is flush so that there is no ridge to catch crumbs. Instead of a conventional handle to lift the top of the refrigerator, there is a suction cup such as you would use to lift plate glass.

The cupboards are arranged so that all plates and cups nest into separate dividers. The liquor locker is custom-designed to fit the particular bottles that are most used onboard.

The dining table is unique in our experience. It utilizes a 3-part articulation system to achieve what is usually done by gimbaling. The advantage is that you avoid having one side of the table, when well heeled, near the overhead and the other side below your knees.

PAPILLON

Photograph by Michael Papo

P*apillon* was custom built as a Great Lakes racing boat. In 1973 she was brought to Florida and converted into a cruising vessel. The modifications have not diminished her sailing performance in the least. From the large center cockpit, you descend the companionway to the main cabin. The bulkheads are white and shiny, giving the impression that everything is "brand new". The master stateroom is aft with its own head and shower. A private starboard passage leads to a single berth and the head and shower for the main cabin. The navigation station is on the port side opposite the single berth. There is a rather comfortable bench with a back rest at the chart table for the navigator. Electronics include complete Brookes and Gatehouse, SSB, VHF Mariner, RDF, Autopilot, and Raytheon Radar.

Papillon's galley forward has appliances including a refrigerator, stove, oven and microwave to port and a double stainless steel sink, counter and stowage to starboard. The counter fiddles are removable for easy cleaning. Convenient also is a dustpan built into the cabin sole with a grating over it.

The main cabin is open to the galley. There are bunks for four people in this saloon, but what you gain in openness you lose in privacy. There is a private cabin in the forepeak.

The chief aesthetic attraction to *Papillon* is how crisp, bright and open she is.

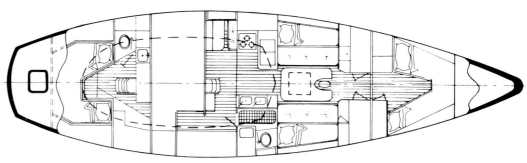

Type:	Yawl
LOA:	57'
LWL:	41'
Beam:	16'
Draft: CBD:	14'
CBU:	6'
Tonnage:	26.8
Designer:	William Tripp
Built:	Russel Bros. Yard, Owen Sound, Ontario, Canada
Year:	1967
Hull:	Aluminum/teak and mahogany trim
Engine:	Detroit Diesel

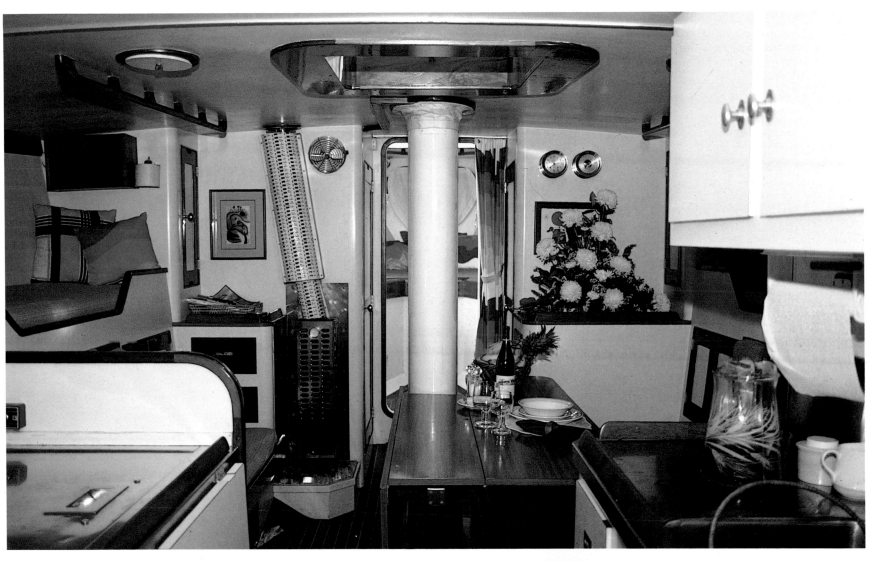

PIGALLE

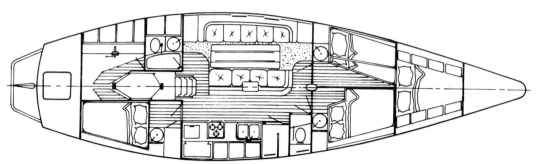

LOA:	48′
Beam:	14½′
Draft: CBU:	4½′
CBD:	9½′
Builder:	Meta-Tarare, La Rochelle, France
Designer:	Michel Joubert
Year:	1978
Hull:	Steel

You don't even have to hear the name to know that this vessel is French. The interior is wildly innovative, as only the French would dare.

Philippe Joubert, the owner and skipper, bought the hull in France and designed the interior himself with the purpose of chartering her in the Caribbean. The main cabin is spacious and totally open. The African ash paneling creates a bright and clean feeling. The centerboard trunk is made useful by incorporating the liquor locker. The saloon settee provides a divider from the galley, which is located amidships on the starboard side. The galley counters are enhanced by beautiful tiles. There is a custom-designed cutting board that fits over the stove and slides neatly away when the stove is in use. Mme. Joubert likes to prepare meals without being excluded from the conversation.

Pigalle can accommodate 6 guests in 3 double cabins. The Jouberts occupy the forepeak. They have purposely sacrificed cabin floor area in order to achieve the maximum width of the double bunks. The theory is that cabins are only for sleeping and stowing clothes, so they would rather reserve all extra space for the communal areas of the boat.

The head is paneled in a sexy black Formica with tile around the basin, cabinet and toilet. There is a full-length mirror on the inside door.

The engine room is as clean and well organized as the rest of the boat. Every tool has a place and remains there when not in use. There is a small built-in workbench to assist in repairs and fabrication.

Forty-eight feet is not particularly large by charter standards, but this delightful French couple has achieved a grand appearance as well as efficiency.

REBEL

We met *Rebel* at Newport, Rhode Island during the 1980 America's Cup. She, like so many others, was taking charter guests out to watch the Twelve Meters compete.

Rebel's interior is all butternut. This wood emanates a rich honey glow, providing both warmth and light to below decks. The owner's stateroom is aft with a double bunk to starboard and a single bunk to port. There is a hanging locker, built-in drawers under the bunks, large bookcase, head with stall shower, and private access via a hatch to the after deck. Forward along the port companionway is a roomy walk-in pantry to port and engine room access to starboard through a full size door. Provision is to be made for foul weather gear storage in the engine room, since there is ample space and engine heat would assist in drying. Currently a separate locker exists for this purpose. Along the starboard side, both forward and aft of the saloon/dining area, are two more double cabins.

The galley, which stretches along the port side, looks beautiful and spacious, but is not very protected for the cook when under sail. Similarly, the large front-loading refrigerator/freezer is not a truly nautical application. Pluses for the galley are the double stainless steel sink with a cutting board designed to fit over it, lots of counter space and stowage. In this galley the cook certainly need not feel left out, being separated from the main saloon only by the back side of the settee. The whole center cabin is spacious and well ventilated. The starboard side overhead hatches open forward and the portside hatches open aft so that when the boat is at a dock the occupants are able to get some air whichever way the wind blows. The mainmast, which you see in the main cabin along the forward bulkhead, is quite original. It is aluminum painted to blend in with the rest of the woody interior. This "trompe l'oeil" effect was created by wiping a ribbed undershirt over the paint. The mast painter even went so far as to add a couple of thumb prints to simulate knots in the wood.

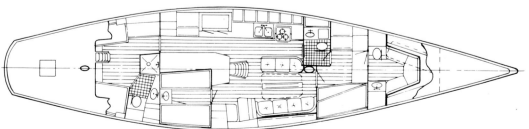

Type:	Ketch
Length:	65'9"
LWL:	47'6"
Beam:	16'1"
Draft:	7'
Builder:	Palmer Johnson
Designer:	McCurdy and Rhodes
Year:	1974
Hull:	Aluminum

ROYONO

Type:	Flush deck racing yawl
LOA:	85'
LOD:	71'
LWL:	53'
Beam:	16'
Draft:	9'
Ballast:	40,000 lbs. lead
Builder:	Nathaniel Herreshoff, Bristol, Rhode Island
Designer:	John Alden
Year:	1936; Rebuilt: 1976-79
Hull:	1¾" mahogany over Swedish steel frames

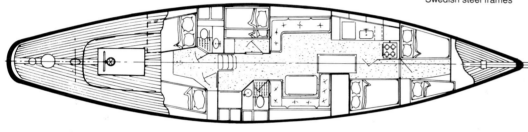

During her early years, *Royono* was a successful ocean racer. In 1950 she was donated to the U.S. Naval Academy and was well known as President John F. Kennedy's favorite sailing yacht. In 1952 she won the Bermuda Race.

Currently she belongs to two young American men, Mike Davis and Geoff Gibson. Geoff skippers her and has spent a lot of time and energy in the last five years rebuilding and restoring *Royono*. Being a do-it-yourself advocate, he recommends Dion's Yard in Salem, Massachusetts for restoration.

Royono is a classic beauty. There is a distinctive red glow emanating from the mahogany paneling that is, perhaps, the combination of the wood and the red velvet upholstery. The cabin sole is cedar. Leaded glass cabinets and brass oil lamps attest to an Old World tradition that is *Royono's* birthright.

The galley is forward in an L-shaped configuration along the port side. Besides the usual fare— stainless steel sink, top-loading icebox built into the wooden counter, gimbaled propane stove and oven—there is an innovative system for visible stowage. On one of the galley bulkheads is a grid with plastic covered wire baskets hooked onto it. These baskets are sturdy and deep enough to stow all kinds of foods and condiments.

An old fashioned feature of *Royono* is a double berth opposite the galley. Traditionally, these are cooks quarters, but there are plans to convert this galley bunk into a more private cabin. Predictably, there is a forward cabin in the fo'c'sle.

Noteworthy on *Royono* is the head. There is an exquisite mahogany sink and cabinet and teak toilet seat—all Geoff's handiwork.

Photograph by Geoff Gibson

86

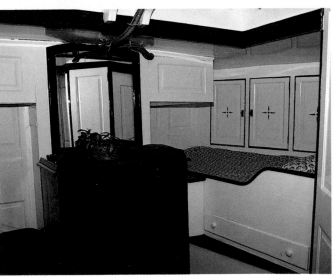

RUGOSA

Rugosa was the fourteenth and last of the NYYC roaring 40s to be built. She is angular, flush and sleek. From her outside lines she looks purely like a racing boat, but her energetic young owners Dennis Buford and Joe Trailer, spent several years rebuilding and renovating her interior so that she is also ideal for cruising.

From the aft cockpit you descend stairs to the aft stateroom where there are two bunks and a chart table. Walking forward to port is the communal head. The main saloon can be entered from either the aft or midship hatch. Old salts and wood boat fanatics would love every aspect of *Rugosa's* interior. The cypress bulkheads are painted eggshell and the exposed mahogany beams are left bright. The sole is yellow pine. The settees are richly upholstered in a dark green wide wale corduroy. Stained leaded glass cabinets and a touch of lace over one of the settees lend an antique look to the main cabin.

The forward galley is tiny but tidy. It's one of those galleys where everything is exposed and within reach. Baskets and net hammocks provide good ventilation for fruits and vegetables. It's handy to have spices and condiments and jarred dry goods visible as long as they are properly secured behind racks, and not in the way of the work space. There is also a convenient knife and icepick holder.

The forepeak could be considered a bit cramped, but it is saved by a large overhead hatch.

Dennis and Joe exemplify the best of the Romantics that one finds tucked away in back water marinas in southern Florida. We have seen many wooden boat enthusiasts determined to "fix it up" and sail around the world. All too few attain their goal. *Rugosa* was lucky that her owners worked hard, were ingenious, and stuck with the job. They made good use of second hand material and found out-of-the-way sources such as Stone Age Antiques in Miami, all of which contributed to a highly individual boat.

Most of the work was done at Riverbend Marina in Fort Lauderdale, one of the better do-it-yourself yards.

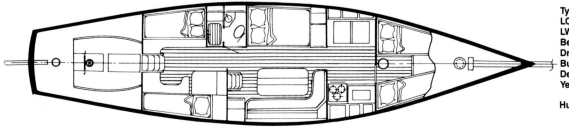

Type:	Yawl
LOD:	59'
LWL:	40'
Beam:	14'6"
Draft:	8'10"
Builder/	Nathaniel Herreshoff
Designer:	Bristol, Rhode Island
Year:	1926
	1979-80 rebuilt
Hull:	Long Leaf yellow pine on oak, bronze fastened

SANDPIPER

Photograph by Bill Page

Bill Page is a yacht broker who lives and carries on business in the picture storybook town of Camden, Maine. A specialty of his is brokering wooden boats. He enjoys his work and takes pride and pleasure in his own lovely wooden boat, *Sandpiper.* Moored in Camden Harbor, *Sandpiper,* as small as she is, is not lost in the midst of the large Windjammer Schooners. Even before going below, a quick look in the cockpit locker gave us a hint of what to expect. All of the lines and sheets are stowed in the locker in a most orderly color-coded fashion on individual pegs. We knew this man had a plan and a place for everything.

The interior is reminiscent of those Creative Playthings that properly use wood in the fabrication of educational toys. A combination of woods make you want to touch everything. The bulkheads are a satin varnished pine; the ceilings and overhead are painted white, and the trim is both butternut and locust. The cabin sole and the ladder are also locust. The galley counter is a varnished cherry, as is the drop-leaf dining table.

Sandpiper sleeps five—two in the V berths in the forepeak and three in the main cabin. There are two pilot berths behind the facing settee and a quarter-berth tucked aft of the galley. The shades and textures of the woods are varied enough so that Page chose a monochromatic approach to his decor. The berths and settees are all done in red. An opening skylight above the dining table contributes brightness to the interior. The galley situated aft near the companionway is similarly well ventilated and a cheery place to work. There is a stainless steel ice chest and sink with a Concordia bronze water pump and coal burning stove. Dish and glass racks and stowage cubbies encircle the working area.

Almost everywhere you look you'll discover some thoughtful small idea. For example, there is a handy holder for the binoculars, and a system by which the depthfinder can swing out and be read from the cockpit and then locked back in place when it is not being used. Another nice detail is the silverware drawer built into the dining table.

Conventional, traditional to be sure, but it is done so well and with such thoughtful attention to detail that it is not at all ordinary.

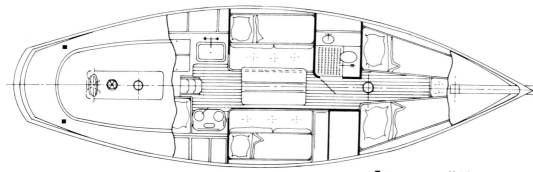

Type:	Ketch
LOA:	34'8"
LWL:	Approximately 27'8"
Beam:	11'
Draft:	5'8"
Headroom:	6'3"
Displ.:	Approximately 22,000 lbs.
Designer:	Winthrop L. Warner
Builder:	Basic boat, Gordon Swift of Exeter, New Hampshire
Year:	1979
Hull:	Carvel Eastern cedar planking over white oak frame and backbone

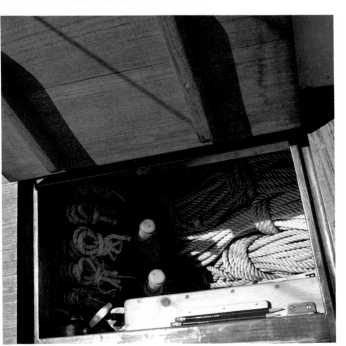

SANDPIPER

SATORI

Photograph by D. Norrie

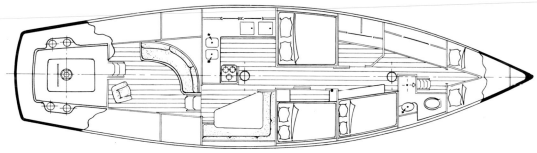

Type:	Gaff Rigged Coastal Schooner
LOA:	75'
LOD:	57'
Beam:	15'
Draft:	8'
Builder/ Designer:	Owners, Ed and Gay Thompson
Year launched:	1975, Wilmington, California
Hull:	Ferrocement
Interior:	Variety of handcrafted hardwoods

Satori is one of our favorite boats. A talented young couple, Ed and Gay Thompson, spent several years designing and building *Satori* in Wilmington, California. Since she was launched in 1975, the Thompsons have spent the last four years chartering her out of St. Thomas, in the Virgin Islands.

The word *Satori* is a zen expression meaning sudden enlightenment. What is so enlightening about this boat is that she transcends all cosmetic conventions that too many designers fall prey to. The interior layout combines both creativity and ingenuity. There is a unique split-level arrangement. Descending from the cockpit, you enter the main saloon on the upper level. The main saloon is a cozy living room environment with a semi-circular couch, Persian rug, sheepskin and pillow lounging area, and even a rocking chair. The bulkheads are constructed of Philippine mahogany and teak. Casting a warm hue to this space is a beautiful stained-glass skylight overhead. Two steps lead you down to the U-shaped galley (on the port side) and the dinette (to starboard). The galley is efficiently arranged so that food may be passed either to the main saloon or the dining area without anyone getting in the cook's way. Also, there is ample counter space with shelves and cubby holes customized to store all sorts of provisions, liquor, and utensils. The dining table has an L-shaped settee and two additional seats that swivel out from under the table when they are needed.

Forward of this area are three oversized double cabins, each one special. They all have built in hanging lockers, shelves, and bookcases. One cabin is finished in Californian redwood, the others employ a little oak, hopia (a type of mahogany), and suli suli. Gay has decorated much of the boat with wood carvings and macramé. The head shared by these cabins is a true work of art. Planked in aromatic cedar, this head is actually a delightful environment! Ed is an advocate of the La Vac head from England. There are gaskets on the seat, a large, sturdy, gusher pump, and no fussing with intake and outlet levers. Ten strokes and you are home free! Opposite the head is a spruce and pine workshop, complete with tool storage. The crews quarters are in the forepeak. *Satori* has 16 opening portholes and six opening hatches. The boat has an exquisite overall ambience. She was conceived and built with love and she shows it.

SCOTCH MIST

Photograph by John Clyde-Smith

Scotch Mist is a motorsailer that manages to avoid the negative connotation of the term. She was designed to sail competitively and she does.

The present owner, a Pennsylvania businessman, changed the name from *Shalimar III* to *Scotch Mist*. The boat is maintained by five liveaboard crew, all English. They are a delightful conscientious group who take enormous pride in their vessel. Skipper John Clyde-Smith and the cook Michael Drury-Beck went out of their way to accommodate us during our interview.

The boat has ample deck space and an enormous pilothouse planked in teak. The main cabin is dramatic, with a happy combination of airiness and elegance. The forward and aft bulkheads are paneled in burled Carpathian elm as is the large dining table to starboard. On the port side are the couch, coffee table, and wicker and leather chairs. The cabin sole is carpeted in a thick plush pile. The large mast, which is covered in leather, successfully impersonates an elegant column. A bar and breakfront are built in and designed to house the cutlery, china and crystal. The fragile items nest securely together and are separated by wooden pegs.

The large windows in the main saloon can be covered by a most interesting and effective shade that pulls up from the bottom. When not in use they reside unobtrusively below the windows.

Aft of the main cabin and four steps below are two private double staterooms port and starboard. They each have their own heads. Both cabins are deliriously decorated with colorful Java print fabric on the bulkheads that matches the bedspreads.

The master stateroom is far aft, extending the full beam of the boat. This luxurious suite has a freestanding kingsize bed against a backdrop of tinted sculpted mirrors. This stateroom also contains its own bar, refrigerator and icemaker. The master head has a His and Her unit joined by a shared marble Jacuzzi bathtub.

Type:	Ketch
LOA:	89'9"
LWL:	82'8"
Beam:	21'
Draft:	9'
Builder:	Stephens Marine, Stockton, California
Designer:	William Garden
Year:	1978
Hull:	Aluminum
Sail Area:	3,943 sq. ft.
Engine:	Twin 330 GT Caterpillar diesels, 250 hp each

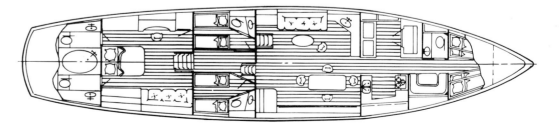

Forward of the main cabin is the galley and the crews quarters. The galley is superbly equipped with a grill, an electric range with oven and microwave also teak cabinets, a double stainless steel sink and a vast counter, inlaid with tile and a butcher block. The cook has all of the right gourmet utensils; Copper Inocuivre pots, Fine carbon steel knives, blenders and Cuisinart, of course.

An interesting galley detail is the cook-designed fiddle system for the stove top. It consists of a stainless steel bracket around the top, drilled with ⅜″ holes to accommodate a rod that can be positioned between any two holes. The rod has a spring on one end which provides the tension that holds it in place. The deep freeze is located beneath the sole, a most efficient location.

Scotch Mist is an elegant yacht with special attention to detail.

SCOTCH MIST

SEA CLOUD

In 1931, when she was launched, *Sea Cloud*, originally named *Hussar*, was the largest private sailing yacht ever built. Commissioned by Edward F. Hutton to be built at Krupp's Germainiawerft Yard in Kiel, she served as a wedding present for Hutton's bride Marjorie Merriwether Post. Their daughter, actress Dina Merrill, virtually grew up on board while *Sea Cloud* traveled worldwide entertaining countless international dignitaries.

Post World War II, *Sea Cloud* had a series of refits costing several million dollars. In the mid 1950's, she was sold to General Trujillo, dictator of the Dominican Republic. Following his assassination in 1961, *Sea Cloud* underwent a variety of ups and downs and assorted owners, resulting in her purchase by Harmut Paschburg and a consortium of German businessmen.

Infused with megafunds and attention, today *Sea Cloud* is in prime condition. Now the ultimate luxury charter yacht, she has scores of staterooms, several deluxe ones with fireplaces, antique furniture, and the kind of opulence found in the best European hotels. With 60 crew, a guest can be assured of first class service. There are banquets fit for royalty at every meal. The house wines served aboard are all very special to go along with the grand atmosphere.

The interior woods are mostly pine, walnut, maple and mahogany. Marble sinks and gold faucets adorn the ships heads. The paneling and moldings are exquisite and the cabins are all accented with lovely carvings and period paintings. *Sea Cloud* is without a doubt a unique sailing experience.

Photograph courtesy of Motor Boating & Sailing

Type:	Four masted schooner
LOA:	353'
LOD:	315'
Beam:	48'11"
Draft:	16'5"
Displacement:	7,780,120 lbs.
Designer:	Stevens & Cox, New York
Buider:	Krupp/Germania Shipyard; Kiel, Germany
Total sail area:	32,280 sq. ft.
Hull:	Steel
Year:	1931
Engine:	Four Enterprise diesels

Photograph by Dan Nerney

104

SERENDY

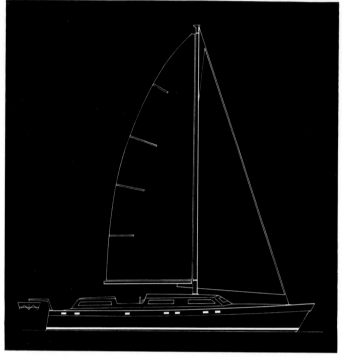

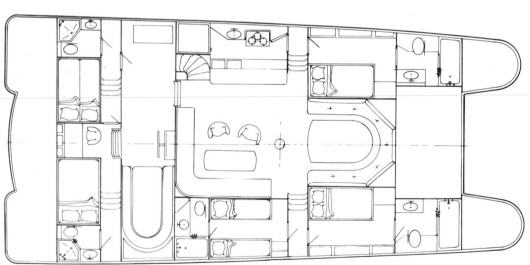

Type:	Catamaran sloop
LOA:	56'
Beam:	25'
Draft:	5'
Builder:	Southampton, England
Designer:	Claude Lagarrigue/ Owner (fashioned after Solaris)
Year:	1978
Hull:	Fiberglass
Engine:	Mercedes diesel 280 hp

Catamarans are incredibly spacious and *Serendy* is certainly no exception. The main saloon looks like a giant living room with a parkay teak sole, a pillowed couch and coffee table to starboard, and a U shaped settee around a large teak dining table against the forward bulkhead. The couch is covered in a jazzy java print cotton fabric and accented with satin pillows. Wicker chests and baskets add a whimsical touch. All of the cabinetry and woodworking are teak.

French owners, Claude and Maryline Lagarrigue and their beautiful young daughter live aboard *Serendy* and operate her as a charter boat. The family occupies the aft cabin which affords them plenty of space and a bit of privacy from their charter guests.

The oak paneled galley is visible from the main saloon. It is situated on the port side, occupying a secure private space, a couple of steps down from the main saloon. Gourmet French cuisine is often passed up to the cockpit for on deck dining.

Three private staterooms each boast oversize double beds, dressing tables, wardrobes and a sea view. They also enjoy connecting heads with showers. There are five heads in total aboard *Serendy*. The head pictured here is attractively finished in polyurethaned cork.

Serendy may look strange if you are used to the sleek lines of monohulls, but she is stable (never rolling more than five degrees) and extremely roomy. *Serendy*; a different way to go!

SILVER HEELS

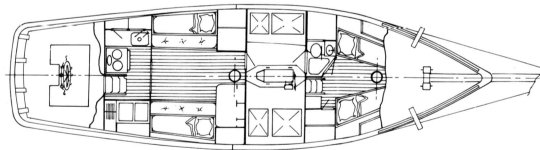

Type:	Schooner
LOA:	41'
Beam:	12'6"
Draft:	6'3"
Designer:	Murray Peterson
Builder:	Camden Ship Building
Year:	1963
Hull:	Philippine mahogany on oak

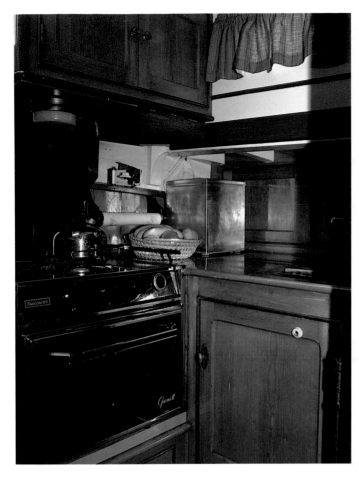

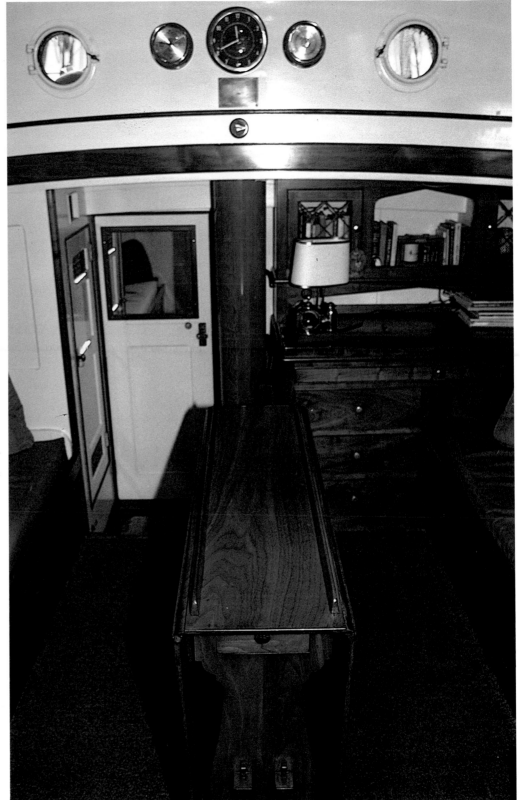

The sprite little schooner, *Silver Heels*, was featured on the cover of the very first issue of *Wooden Boat* magazine in 1974. True to Maine ship building tradition, she is exquisitely well put together. Her owner, Howland Jones of Harwichport, Massachusetts, maintains her in bristol condition. The layout is not unusual for an aft cockpit boat. What is special is the detailed workmanship, the curved archways, the combination chart table/ chest, with decorative bookcase and stained glass cupboards, which singles *Silver Heels* out as being uniquely a Murray Peterson design. The interior is painted a crisp white and accented by black walnut trim. There is a generous portion of bright work in the galley. The black propane stove provides a strong aesthetic contrast to the wood.

The main saloon is simple and functional without being too austere. There are no nicknacks or personal affectations scattered around. Because of the ultra tidiness of this boat, the details of the woodworking are all the more evident. The cabin sole is carpeted in the same forest green color in which the settees are upholstered.

There is a beautiful handcrafted deckbox built to hold the propane tanks in a horizontal position.

We found *Silver Heels* anchored in South Bristol, Maine, in front of the Peterson compound, looking very much as if she belonged to the beautiful, but rugged Maine coastline.

SOUQUI

Souqui is the "queen" of all the houseboats residing in Paris. Earlier in her career, *Souqui* hauled cargo between Europe and Indonesia via the Cape of Good Hope. In 1935, she was converted by an Englishman to more or less yacht standards. After changing hands a half a dozen times, she was purchased by Michel Destandau, a French interior decorator and antique collector. He resides on her in a prime Parisian location; facing the Quai Conti just below the Mazarine Library and opposite the Louvre and the Palais Royal. *Souqui* is capable of sailing in open waters but must keep her spars stepped to travel under the low bridges which span the River Seine.

Her hull is black and intriguingly curvacious near the bow. Her decks are painted red and her hatches are finished bright. The interior is filled with exotica. Below, she is replete with treasures; engraved chests, paintings, suits of armor, figureheads, statuettes, and countless other oddities that would be perfectly at home in a museum. The character of the main saloon, heads, and galley indicate a unique sense of humor. Michel enjoys his noteriety. Where would he stow everything if he took off for across the Atlantic?

Photographs by Allan Weitz

Photograph by Allan Weitz

Photograph by Allan Weitz

Photograph by Allan Weitz

Type:	Dutch river barge
Length:	79′
Beam:	approx. 18′
Built:	Gronigen, Holland
Hull:	Steel
Year:	1890

Photograph by Allan Weitz

Photograph by Allan Weitz

Photograph by Allan Weitz

SOUTHERLY

Photographed by Michael Koppstein

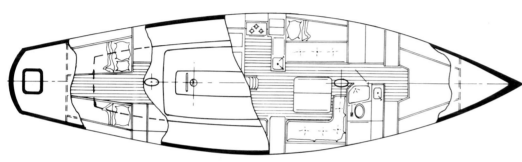

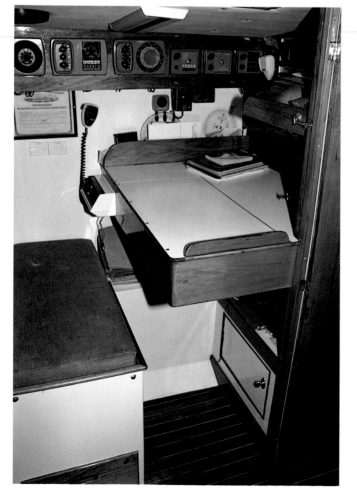

Type:	Ketch
LOA:	55′7″
LWL:	42′6″
Beam:	14′
Draft:	CBU 5′2″
Designer:	Sparkman & Stephens, Inc.
Builder:	Paul Luke, East Boothbay, Maine
Year:	1974
Hull:	Aluminum alloy

Southerly, designed as a racing vessel, modified for cruising at Minnefords Yard in Long Island, New York in 1978, is currently a charter yacht operating out of St. Thomas. Her list of specifications; S & S designed, Paul Luke built, imply a most "proper yacht." Layout is conventional with a small cabin aft of the cockpit for the crew. In the main cabin the galley is a crisp and compact U configuration to port and contains a Grunert deep freeze and a three-burner stove with oven. Opposite the galley, the navigation area, replete with Brookes and Gatehouse, is equally neat and efficient. The bulkheads are a starched looking white with mahogany trim, and the cabin sole is predictably teak and holly. However, Southerly has a certain "something" which defies further stereotyping.

We attribute this "something" to the judicious use of butternut, a member of the walnut family. The

handcrafted cabinets, settee trim, and saloon table are rich without being overbearing or dark. The settee trim and the table are inlaid with mahogany and elm. The settees, portside pilot berths and navigator's seat are all upholstered in a taupe cotton blend washable fabric which complements the honey blonde woodwork. Colorful pillows and a burgundy toned Persian rug accent the main saloon.

Modifications to the interior included replacing the entire overhead with removable panels for easy access to the deck fittings. Also, in order to enlarge the living/lounging space, a starboard bunk was sacrificed to a curved settee area with increased stowage. The new table is both decorative and versatile. It raises, lowers, flips over, pulls out and the extension rests on a folding leg.

The overall subtle effect of Southerly's interior is enhanced by indirect rheostat lighting.

113

STARBOUND

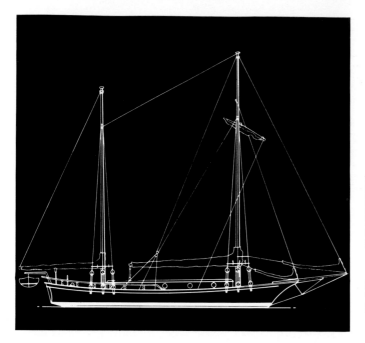

Type:	Auxiliary ketch
LOA:	68'
LOD:	50'
Beam:	17½'
Draft:	6'3"
Displacement:	35 tons
Builder:	Bahr Bros. Shipyard, Atlantic Highlands, New Jersey
Designer:	William J. Deed
Year:	1950
Hull:	Long leaf yellow pine on double oak frames

Gordon and Nina Stuermer and their son, Ernie, moved aboard *Starbound* in 1966, and began their education about sailboats. In 1973, the family left their berth in Annapolis, Maryland and proceeded to circumnavigate the world, returning to the States in 1976. *Starbound* contains a compendium of artifacts and small treasures procured from international ports. The interior is exotically eclectic. The woods are butternut, white walnut, teak and mahogany. The aft saloon, with its corduroy couches, cabinets and bookshelves, is quite homey. Nina took the time to show us her shell collection, souvenirs, and teak carvings done by a young friend in Bali.

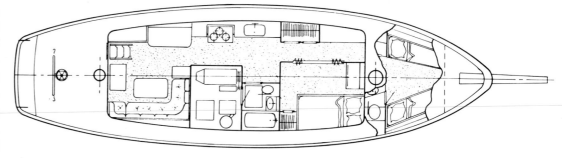

The galley is admidship with a propane range, stainless steel sink and counter area and stowage nooks and crannies everywhere. The Steurmers' cabin is forward of the gallery, featuring a large double bunk and a mask to ward off evil spirits. Ernie's, cabin is in the fo'c'sle. There are true accommodations for four. If another couple joins the Stuermers, then Ernie sleeps in the main saloon or rigs a hammock topsides. The master head has a shower and bathtub.

Gordon and Nina were in Deltaville, Virginia, when we encountered them. They were up in the ways preparing for their second round-the-world voyage, hoping to leave before the end of 1981.

This gregarious couple has written two books on their experiences. The first, *Starbound* is an account of their circumnavigation; the second is called, *Deep Water Cruising* and contains much practical nautical information.

THE STING

Since its inception, the Freedom 40 has received a lot of press. Apparently the wishbone rig is extremely efficient and simple to use. This very different-looking boat is also quite fast. Owners Roland and Maram absolutely adore *The Sting* and find it an ideal charter boat for the Caribbean. With the centerboard they can anchor in shallow water near beautiful reefs. The rig is so easy to set up, there is no problem stopping in one bay for lunch and hoisting sail and checking out a new anchorage for the cocktail hour. The large cockpit is conducive to entertaining and sunning, and the completely separate aft cabin (head and shower) allows for maximum privacy.

Amidships is the saloon dining area with a colorful, curved settee and a round teak table. The galley is L-shaped, with a double stainless steel sink and a Grunert refrigerator/freezer. Bright yellow and red plastic racks enable utensils and canisters of tea, pasta, and sugar to hang from the galley walls.

An additional cabin and head and shower are forward. Both heads are Wilcox Crittendon with Electra San treatment. If another bunk is required, the dining settee converts to a three-quarters berth.

The Sting seems to offer clean-cut, low maintenance fun.

Photograph by Roland Hanel

Type:	Cat ketch
LOA:	44'
LOD:	40'
LWL:	35'
Beam:	12'
Draft:	3'6" CBU
Builder:	Tillotson-Pearson, Rhode Island
Designer:	Gary Hoyt
Year:	1978
Hull:	Fiberglass

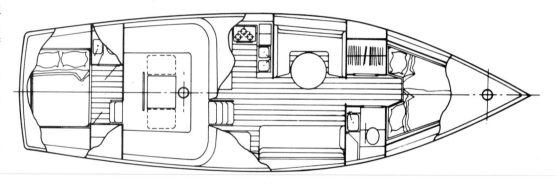

TABOR BOY

Tabor Boy was originally designed as a North Sea training ship. She has undergone some changes, but remains true to her tradition in the service of Tabor Academy in Marion, Massachusetts. All of the work on board is done by the students, under the direction of Captain Glaeser. Repairs, whether woodworking or mechanical, are part of the training program. For ten months at a stretch, 22 students live, learn and work aboard.

In 1950, Tabor Boy had a major refit including a new deckhouse by DeVries Lynch. The deckhouse entrance with its twin portholes and benches is especially attractive.

Below is an enormous main saloon with a library, fireplace and dining facilities for a couple of dozen hungry mates. The galley has a commercial walk-in refrigerator and a large South Bend propane stove.

With traditional older boats such as Tabor Boy such things as windlasses and capstans must either be fabricated or imported from Europe. Captain Glaeser said that many hard-to-find items are also available at Lunenberg Foundry, Nova Scotia.

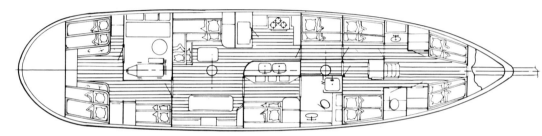

Type:	Training Schooner
LOA:	92'
Beam:	22'
Draft:	10'6"
Builder/ Designer:	The Netherlands government
Year:	1914; converted to a yacht in 1950
Hull:	Wrought Iron

TANTRA SCHOONER

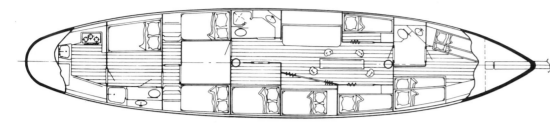

Photograph by Reid Stowe

Type:	Schooner
LOA:	80'
LOD:	70'
Beam:	16½'
Displacement:	90 tons
Builder/	
Designer:	Owner Reid Stowe, built in Cape Fear, North Carolina
Year:	1978
Hull:	Steel and fiberglass

Tantra Schooner is a one-of-a-kind boat. Owner Reid Stowe, an artist and a sculptor, is quite an adventurer. Before building *Tantra Schooner*, he traveled extensively on a small 27 foot, 1,400-lb. catamaran to Europe, Africa, Southern Brazil, and up the Amazon.

Built with the help of Reid's brothers, Bob and Hank, *Tantra Schooner* has been a culmination of Reid's experiences and dreams. He loves tropical exotic woods; he spent a lot of time acquiring them in Dominica, Surinam and Guyana. The boat boasts twenty different kinds of woods, among them, saman, red cedar, mahogany, gomier, purple heart, silver bali and numerous lesser known native woods of South America such bordemeer, carob peat, and lawi pueb. The spelling may be wrong, but at least the sound of the word is close.

When Reid finished the exterior, he left North Carolina for the Caribbean with his wife, Iris, and two-month-old daughter, Viva. He finished the interior *en route* and in the islands.

Most of the interior paneling is sculpted in bas relief. There is one panel where Iris' handiwork can be seen: beautiful carved walnut inlaid with enamel.

Tantra Schooner is an unusual design with a lifetime plan built in. *Tantra* is now working as a charter boat. The charter accommodations are fabricated so that when extra quarters are not necessary, that space is set up to be a cargo hold— the intent being to make *Tantra Schooner* totally self supporting.

Reid and Iris are a delightful, spiritual couple. Their boat reflects their ingenuity, creativity, and joy of life.

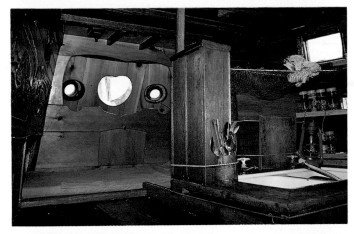

TAR BABY

Type:	Schooner
LOA:	60'
LOD:	50'
Draft:	7'2"
Beam:	14'
Builder:	C. A. Morse & Son, Thomaston, Maine
Designer:	John G. Alden
Year:	1928
Hull:	Hard pine over oak

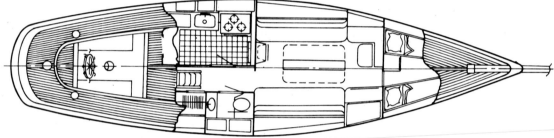

In 1928, Mr. Hood of Hood Dairies commissioned *Tar Baby* to be built. It was a long marriage. Mr. Hood kept *Tar Baby* until 1975. She is currently owned by Carl Sherman of Westbrook, Connecticut, who takes pride in maintaining this classic gem in the style to which she has become accustomed.

Unusual for an Alden design, the galley is aft with a passthrough to the cockpit. The galley is almost like a small private cabin, totally separate from the rest of the boat.

The main saloon emanates charm and Old World elegance; white paint relieved with mahogany accents, stained glass cabinets, a fireplace, and oil lamps. Pullman bunks fold unobtrusively flush to the bulkhead when not in use. They then act as back rests for the settees.

The chart table is unusual in that it pulls down from the forward bulkhead of the main saloon.

The forward cabin is small, but pleasant. In order to increase ventilation, an omni-directional wind-scoop attached to the skylight is used.

Tar Baby, as old as she is, is not retired. She makes a habit of joining all of the usual schooner and wooden boat races around New England in the summertime. It's a good thing that *Tar Baby* has fallen into loving hands. She is a sweetheart and deserves attention.

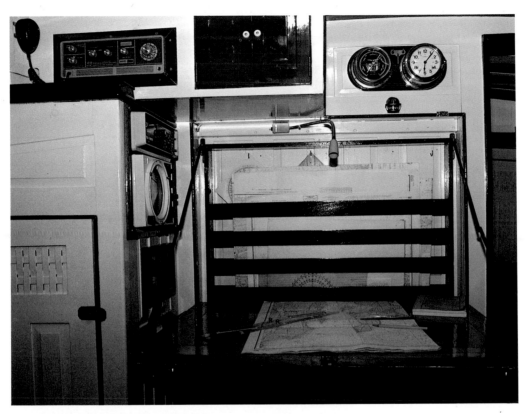

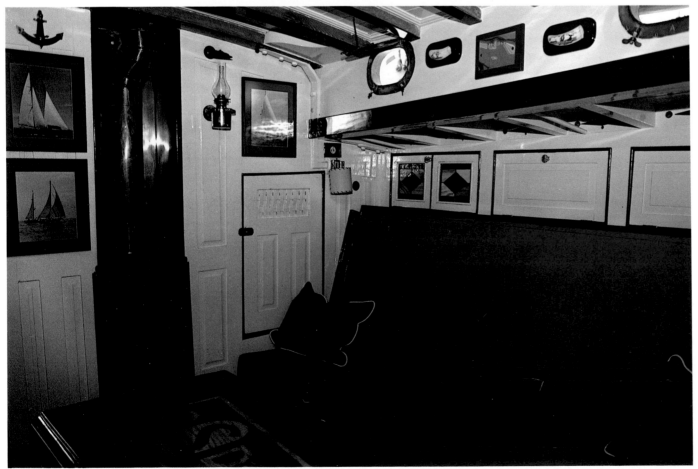

TAR BABY

125

TICONDEROGA

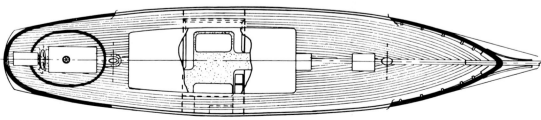

Type:	Ketch
LOA:	85′
LOD:	72′
LWL:	68′9″
Beam:	16′
Draft:	7′10″
Displacement:	119,016 lb.
Builder:	Quincy Adams Yacht Yard, Quincy, Massachusetts
Designer:	L. Francis Herreshoff
Year:	1936
Hull:	Double planked mahogany
Total sail area:	2,800 sq. ft.
Engine:	GMC 130 hp

Ticonderoga is a powerful old Indian name and the boat is certainly worthy of it. She is one of the most famous American yachts, known for her beauty and her exceptional sailing performance. During her career as a racing vessel, she accomplished the feat of holding over 30 major ocean race records at one time; that, in itself, a record.

From 1967-68, *Ticonderoga* was rebuilt and designed for charter work. She now accommodates six guests in three double staterooms, each with private access to heads and showers.

The skipper and mate share a private cabin and head, and there are uppers and lowers in the forepeak, with a private entrance for steward and deckhand. The forward galley has a large double stainless steel sink with a cutting board that fits over one side. The main mast, which is stepped to the keel, provides a steadying pillar for the cook. There is a large refrigerator with long, deep shelves, and front-loading access. The galley has plenty of stowage and work space, but unfortunately it has an electric stove and oven. The generator must be on even to make a cup of coffee. A deep freeze unit is part of a built-in unit in the main saloon.

The cabins off the central long and narrow companionway have large double berths with stowage cubbies as their base and built-in drawers under the bunks, as well as hanging lockers.

The carpeted main saloon has a large mahogany gimbaled table and a U-shaped settee around it.

One of the most extraordinary things about *Big Ti* is her beautiful deck, cockpit, and distinctive gold leaf dolphins punctuating her rails.

Ken and Fran MacKenzie, owners of *Ticonderoga*, spent the early years of their marriage operating her themselves as a charter boat. These days, two children later, Fran has opted for a life ashore in Newport, Rhode Island. Even though Ken has had a few skippers work for him, he never seems to tire of skippering *Ti* himself.

Ken is proud of his vessel and always rises to a competitive situation. He takes great pleasure in showing off *Ti's* racing prowess. By the way, *Ticonderoga* never did collide with the other boat pictured here during the 1980 Classic Boat Regatta in Newport.

VANDA

V*anda* is an exquisite sailing vessel with a turn of the century flair. Her graceful teak decks seem to stretch forever—still there is a protective deckhouse for the helmsman. Dining on deck is a pleasant tradition aboard *Vanda*.

To enter the mail saloon you descend the companionway via a handsome, albeit steep, staircase with decorously carved handrail. The main saloon is veritably gleaming with its French polished mahogany panels and pewter place setting. Teak trim accents the woodwork. The built-in Victorian settees are upholstered in striped blue velvet cloth. In fact, royal blue seems to be a major theme aboard *Vanda* judging from the color of the carpet, bedspreads, tablecloth, napkins, and pillows.

Old fashioned glassed-in cupboards, a beautiful fireplace with an inlaid panel overhead, scrolled doorknobs, and matching lamps on the bulkhead further accentuate *Vanda*'s Old World charm.

Owners Paul and Jeannie Drinkwine and their West Indian crew Sam and Fernando operate *Vanda* as a charterboat in the Caribbean. The accommodations include three private double staterooms and separate crews quarters. All of the drawers and cabinets are finely crafted to fit tightly. Workmanship aboard *Vanda* indicates both an eye towards aesthetics and function.

Even though she is an older wooden boat, *Vanda* has been renovated so that the galley is fully modern with refrigerator/freezer. The heads are electric and there is hot and cold pressure water in the two showers; a representative of a bygone era enters the twentieth century.

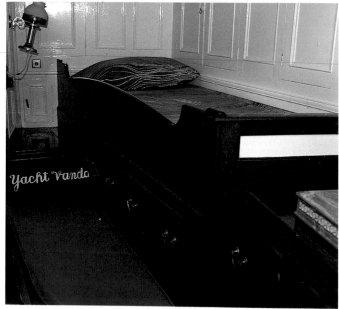

Type:	Ketch
LOA:	93'
LOD:	87'
Beam:	16' 6"
Draft:	9' 9"
Builder/ Designer:	H. Stowe & Son, Shoreham by the Sea, England
Year:	1909: Rerigged: 1930: Renovations: 1978
Tonnage:	81 Tm
Engine:	GMC 671 Diesel, 225 HP
Hull:	Teak on English grown oak frames

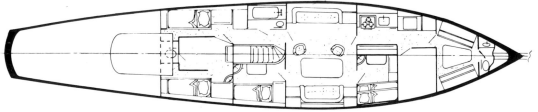

VICTORIA

Victoria is a sister ship to *Ticonderoga*. Her interior is totally different. In fact, below decks *Victoria* is completely unique! Owners John and Susi Barkhorn of Honolulu and Santa Barbara, California, commissioned Joe Artese of Laguna Beach to redesign the interior.

The master stateroom aft is paneled in walnut and includes a handsome built-in chest of drawers with brass handles and a queen size berth. The master head has a marble bathtub and Jacuzzi adorned with a tile mosaic on the bulkhead behind' it. The sink, sculpted like a scallop shell is adorned with a gilded faucet.

There is a customized, elaborate cupboard along the companionway for just about every flag in the manual. The woods in the main saloon are walnut and cherry. When we first entered the saloon, the woodwork fairly took our breath away. Also, the opulence of the burgundy velvet settees, the mirrors, the brass lamps and fireplace are all dazzling. Some of the cabinets are caned for ventilation. The horizontal surfaces have brass rails around them to act as fiddles. Forward, the galley and crews quarters are paneled in teak.

In 1981, *Victoria* sailed from Palm Beach to Monte Carlo and the Mediterranean. There is a full-time skipper aboard, and the Barkhorns and their young son, Charles, join the boat when they are able.

Victoria is, perhaps, the most sophisticated yacht we have seen in the sense that she combines an individual and unconventional elegence below without nautical compromise.

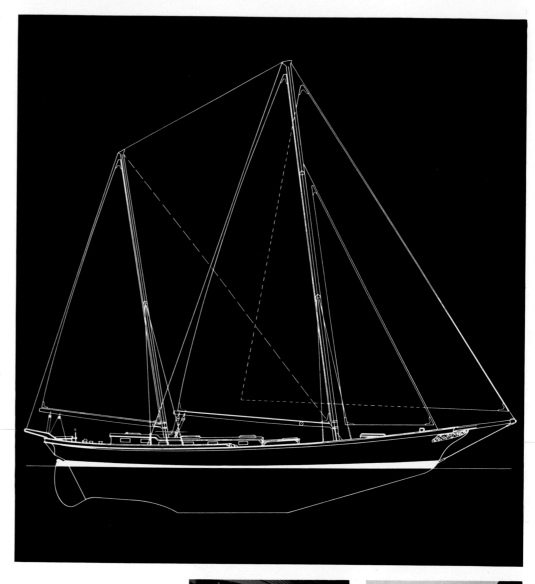

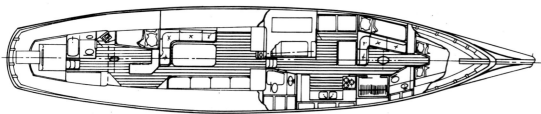

Type:	Ketch
Length:	72'
Beam:	16'
Draft:	7'9"
Displacement:	108,288 lb.
Builder:	P. Vos Ltd., Auckland, New Zealand
Designer:	L. Francis Herreshoff
Year:	1974; Interior redesigned in California— completed 1978
Hull	Cold molded constructed with epoxy, Kaori wood
Sail area:	2,897 sq. ft.

130

VOLCANO

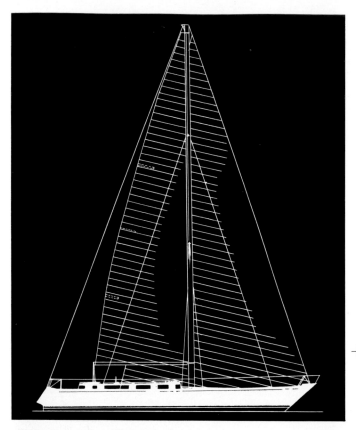

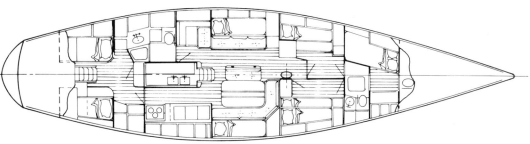

Type:	Sloop
Length:	62'2"
LWL:	50'
Beam:	16'6"
Draft:	7'
Displacement:	58,000 lb.
Builder:	Bob Derecktor, Mamaroneck, New York
Designer:	German Frers
Year:	1978
Hull:	Aluminum
Sail Area:	1,798.25 sq. ft.
Engine:	Perkins 6.354 diesel

Volcano was custom built and designed for Llwyd Ecclestone, Jr. of Florida, who wanted a comfortable, well-equipped family cruiser that could be raced under the IOR rule. As a result, *Volcano* is fast, stable and nicely laid out with three private staterooms, congenial main saloon, two heads with showers and, of course, hot and cold running water.

The galley is admidships and runs fore and aft with a range oven, two compartment refrigerator and large deep freeze. A special fresh water dispenser is connected to the refrigeration system and allows a cold drink anytime. There is a hidden stainless steel garbage container, always a good idea aboard a boat. The cook showed us her system for keeping crackers and biscuits from getting soggy: an electric brisker, operating 12-32/110V emits a small amount of heat to keep things crisp.

Tho main saloon is bright and cheerful, with a large dining table and plenty of stowage behind the settees. The cabinets are well ventilated with wicker work. In fact, the whole boat is well ventilated with ten deck hatches, ten seaside opening portholes, and 12 fans for cooling off in the tropics. For cold weather, *Volcano* has warm air heating throughout.

The navigation and radio equipment are state of the art, including two Loran Cs, RDF, single side-band, weatherfax, two logs, knotmeter, wind guide and wind speed indicators, VHF, and HF radio transceivers.

Individual cubbyholes, typical of a racing boat, abound, and prove useful for cruising.

Service manuals are readily accessible in looseleaf binders, just another indication of the high level of organization aboard *Volcano*.

In addition to racing and family cruising, *Volcano* is also available for charter at various times both in the Caribbean and in New England. She carries with her an inflatable speedboat as well as a pair of Windsurfers. *Volcano* is the culmination of a series of boats that Mr. Ecclestone has had built for himself. He has been striving for perfection and comes closer every time.

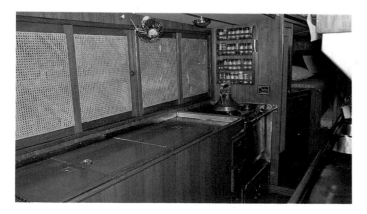

MAIN SALOONS

We are including a whole separate section on main saloons to indicate that there are many different configurations to which you can apply some basic rules.

The main saloon is the living room, dining room, study and den all rolled into one. Furthermore, it must be dry, but well ventilated; cozy, but with at least a feeling of spaciousness; comfortable, but with no compromise to safety. That most achieve these occasionally contradictory goals is a tribute to thoughtful designers and ingenious owners.

The traditional skylight, lovely to look at, must usually be closed in wet weather and, even then, is a likely leaker. A reversible Plexiglas hatch cover seems to admit the most air and light and the least water. The more opening ports there are, the better. Leakage can be kept to a minimum by attention to the gasket, care not to overtighten and judicious use of sealant. All opening ports and hatches should be fitted with an insect screen.

A boat need not be 50 feet to have an attractive main saloon. We know a 25-foot boat, *Plumbelly* (page 139), with a most comfortable main cabin. Four seated for dinner on the handsome leather cushions around a large wooden table aglow from the oil lamp have all the room they need—and everything is within reach.

For more conventional saloons, it may be useful to note that a settee should be a minimum of 20 inches wide and its back angled outward. The height above the sole should not exceed 16 inches. If a table is used in conjunction with the settee, it should be 10-12 inches above the settee top. Tables can be made to gimbal, articulate, fold away, extend, raise and lower and convert to a bunk. Some have built-in stools that swing out on the opposite side from the settee to accommodate additional diners.

Handholds and grabrails should be such that you are never out of reach of one and secure enough for a 300 pounder to hold on without loosening it. Round all edges and corners to prevent potentially nasty injuries.

The following photographs are an indication of how many different ways a main saloon can be arranged. Design, decor, and detail are all so important. The main saloon embodies the essence of a yacht's interior. Whether traditional or modern, the ambiance sets the tone for life on board.

Eudroma

Cyrano

Eudroma is a 64-foot ketch designed by Fred Shepherd and built at Shoreham-by-the-Sea, England in 1937 of pitchpine on black oak. Her main saloon was newly decorated by the present owners Tim and Louella Holsten. There is a striped L shaped settee around a gimbaled oak dining table. An Old World ambiance pervades.

Cyrano is a 77-foot motorsailer, built in 1963 in the Abacos in the Bahamas. Her hull was constructed of native pine over horseflesh and dogwood. Formerly, William Buckley's boat, she is now owned by Robert Johns of Fort Lauderdale. Her main saloon is unusually laid out to include a piano!

Taipi II is a 45-foot staysail schooner built 1977 in Cannes, France, and designed by Peter Ibold. The hull is ferrocement and the interior trim and dining table are mahogany. Parisian, Alain Schiller, loves the saloon/galley combination. There is an elegant U shaped settee around a fixed table that does not convert to a bunk. Two chairs can be folded up and stowed when under way.

Tantra is a 75-foot motorsailer ketch owned by E. Taylor Chewning of Washington, D.C. She was built in 1978 of aluminum at the Palmer Johnson yard in Sturgeon Bay, Wisconsin. Her main saloon adapts well to lounging or dining. Pictured here, the table is lowered to coffee table level and the rattan chairs are to starboard. The table can be raised to dining level and the chairs drawn up to it. The fireplace provides a pleasant focal point for the saloon.

Taipi II

Tantra

Alkyone

Blue Jacket

Raanga

Blue Jacket (ex Robin) was Ted Hood's personal 52-foot ocean racing yawl in 1972. She was built in Holland, of Airex core fiberglass by Franz Maas to Hood's specifications. The main saloon is compartmentalized; dining, lounging, galley, navigation station and an extra berth are all communally located. There is a library and a two sectioned teak table. *Blue Jacket* is now owned by Henry Sanson of West Hartford, Connecticut.

Raanga, a 72-foot steel schooner built in 1976 at Chantiers Navals de Boit, Antibes, France, was designed by Carlo Sciarelli. The aft cabin is the main saloon. This cabin is paneled in birch and the unusual V shaped table is mahogany. On the aft bulkhead are two steps for an emergency entrance through the hatch.

Alkyone is a Swan 57 designed by Sparkman and Stephens and built in 1979 by Nautor in Finland. Her main saloon is spacious with a large dining table and curved settee to starboard. The bulkheads are paneled in teak veneer. Rounded archways between cabins are indicative of Nautor built boats.

Wind Dancer is a Cherubini 44 built of fiberglass in 1979 in Burlington, New Jersey designed *à la* Herreshoff. One of the nicest production boats we have seen, her main saloon is paneled in solid mahogany. *Wind Dancer* is owned by Martin Williams of Toms River, New Jersey. The main saloon is light and airy with a skylight overhead that can be turned to provide windscoop ventilation. The port settee opens to create a double berth. All of the hanging lockers and cupboards have cane work for ventilation. The opening ports are cleverly designed, angled such that they provide ventilation even in a heavy rain.

Freespirit is a 76-foot cutter, designed by Bruce King and built at Willards in southern California of Airex foam core. This innovative cutter was completed in 1980 and is owned by Californian Harlan Lee. The main saloon has a lounging and entertainment center, separate from the dinette. The coffee table and cabinets are African mahogany. The settees are attractively covered in forest green ultra suede. A wet bar pulls down on hinges.

New Horizons is a 60-foot auxiliary cruising ketch designed by Stan Huntingford, built in Vancouver of ferrocement and launched in 1974. This unusual boat is a fine example of good joinery work. The interior paneling is teak. This main saloon is forward of the galley and the two double cabins. The mahogany table is beautifully crafted to extend for additional guests. Bryan Fleming skippers *New Horizons*.

New Horizons

Wind Dancer

Free Spirit

137

Active

Elinor

Active is a 43-foot schooner built in Robin Hood, Maine in 1963 and designed by Murray Peterson. Her owners are Bruce Mastersen and Marcia Barthelme. Her hull is mahogany on oak and bronze fastened; the interior is mahogany with rock maple sole. The main saloon features a decorative alcove and cabinet with leaded glass panes. The settee backrest lifts to create additional bunks. It's a very tidy saloon.

Elinor is a three-masted Danish Baltic Trader, built in Stubbekøbing, Denmark in 1906. Her hull is oak, decks are pitch pine, and yang teak and her spars are Oregon pine. Skippered by Pelle Blinkenberg, this fine vessel was rebuilt from 1971-78. Her main saloon is rustic and stark, but a boat of this size carries so many people that the brightness comes easily from the number of guests who sit down to a meal together.

Galadriel

Adventure

Freedom

Plumbelly

Galadriel is a 37-foot steel cruising boat (seen on page 174). The main saloon is replete with personal touches; a macrame holder suspends the oil lamp, stained glass and lots of pictures adorn the bulkheads. The tiled fireplace adds warmth.

Freedom: This 60-foot Nova Scotia schooner was built in 1970 and refurbished from 1975-78. The hull is black spruce on oak and the paneling in the galley/saloon area featured here is cedar and pine. In the work boat tradition, there is no formal saloon other than the dinette in the aft galley.

Adventure, the 121-foot Windjammer Schooner, designed by Thomas McMannis, and built in 1926 in the James Yard in Essex, Massachusetts is owned and skippered by Capt. Jim Sharp of Camden, Maine. The hull is planked and framed in oak, with hard pine ceilings and decks. The interior aft saloon is paneled in maple. *Adventure* was one of the last of the Gloucester fishing schooners. Her saloon with its wood-burning stove and antique nautical artifacts on the bulkheads is beautifully preserved.

Plumbelly is a 25-foot 'round the world cruising boat handbuilt of tropical woods in Bequia by owner Klaus Alverman. As small as she is, the main saloon is quite cozy even for a small dinner party. Leather cushions on the cabin sole act as settees and a wooden storage box doubles as a dining table.

Shearwater

Mary Day

Wrestler

Shearwater a 62-foot ketch designed by John Alden was built in 1928 at the Reed Cook Construction Co. in Boothbay, Maine. The interior was totally redone 1979-80. The main saloon incorporates Philippine and Honduras mahogany and some teak and cedar. A lot of thought went into the main cabin details such as tape stowage. *Shearwater* has a spacious yet cozy feeling.

Wrestler is a 1926 tug boat built of yellow pine over oak, in Brookline, New York. She is owned by Philip Sanborn of W. Boothbay, Maine. Her main saloon has a whimsical charm with stained glass windows and velvet settee. You can peer down to the Cooper Bessemer 4 cylinder diesel from behind the settee.

Mary Day is an 83-foot Windjammer Schooner built in 1962 of oak at the Harvey Gamage Yard in South Bristol, Maine. Her skipper/owner Havilah S. Hawkins designed her interior expressly for "Head Boat" charters, i.e., to accommodate large groups who come on board as individuals to meet others and share a sailing experience. The companionway stairs are meant to facilitate entry by older people. The fireplace and organ (not pictured here) lend a feeling of a country inn to the main saloon.

Bride of Gastonia is a 45-foot Seth Persson, built in Old Saybrook, Connecticut. Owned by Frank Eberhart of New York. Her main saloon paneled in teak and a light ash, she is traditional with her gimbaled centerline dining table, port and starboard settees and pilot berth. She sports a Paul Luke stove, there is a folding door between the saloon and the forepeak.

Athena is an 80-foot ketch designed by Dave Dana and custom built by Bill Rudolph in Miami, Florida in 1969. Skipper/owner Bob Roulette, an Irish Canadian, operates Athena in the Virgin Islands as a charterboat. The hull is triple planked diagonal cedar. The main saloon takes up the entire aft section of the boat. The double-sized pilot berth behind the dining table is also a colorful lounging alcove. The table is mahogany and the cabin sole is pine. Windows in the transom add a tremendous amount of light.

Athena

MAIN SALOONS

Viking is a 40-foot ketch designed by Nelson Zimmer and built in Risør, Norway in 1966; the same yard where Colin Archers were built. Her hull is constructed of teak on white oak frames. Joe Giovino, the owner has sailed, by his own accounting, half way around the world on this vessel. Her main saloon is traditional and handsome with leather covered settees and lovely teak paneling.

Alegria is a 64-foot custom cruising ketch, designed by Philip Rhodes, and constructed of steel by Kok shipyard in Muiden, Holland. She is skippered by Bruce Bodine and his wife Sharon. The main saloon, a couple of steps below the pilothouse, is light and airy, with plenty of windows and portholes.

Viking

Alegria

Mattie

Linda

Argyll

Linda is a 48-foot Baltic, built of oak in 1903 in Denmark for fishing. She is now a pleasure craft, renovated by owners the Van Perreras of St. Maarten. Her main saloon is furnished with imports from Afghanistan, Turkey and Indonesia. The little pooch looks quite comfortable, but who wouldn't be?

Argyll is a 58-foot Sparkman and Stephens yawl built of mahogany in 1948. She was recently renovated by owner Stan Parks of Camden, Maine. Her main saloon is traditional in that it is painted white with mahogany trim. Two pilot berths sit above the settees both port and starboard. Besides being useful as sea berths, they add a new dimension to the main saloon space.

Mattie is a turn of the century fishing schooner which is now a Windjammer boat. Her interior is not very opulent but the wood paneling is exquisite.

Sherpa

Paradise

Quicksilver

Vixen

Sherpa is a 60-foot catamaran built of fiberglass in Southampton, England in 1978. The interior was finished in St. Malo, France by the owner Rene Alexandre. The main saloon is like a contemporary lounge with bean bag chairs and coffee table.

Quicksilver is a 47-foot trimaran ketch designed by Norm Cross and built in 1976 of mahogany in Capetown, South Africa. A 27-foot beam yields the space to have double bunks on either side of the main saloon, which can be closed off with curtains. The saloon is open to the galley with a dinette to port and a settee to starboard.

Paradise is a 50-foot Gulfstar custom sloop, built in 1979, for charter. She has a fiberglass hull with a teak veneer interior. The main saloon is straightforward—a congenial arrangement for cook and guests. The bright white threaded material on the settee is machine washable and easily removed by zippers.

Vixen is a New York 40 built originally in 1916 by Herreshoff. She was rebuilt and thoroughly renovated from 1968-78. Her dining table is butternut, the settees are leather, and the design behind the tables is onyx.

Stardust is a 47-foot Greiger design sailboat. Her hull is cedar on oak, her decks are teak and her interior has mahogany trim. This keyhole view of the main saloon allows us a glimpse of a double berth to starboard and a settee and pilot berth to port. The dining table is accessible from both sides when it is raised. The bunks look comfortable for lounging and sleeping but there are no back rests for sitting.

Lusty is a 62-foot ketch designed by William Tripp and built of fiberglass in Newport Beach, California. The main saloon is finished in teak and formica. The table top is Baltic birch. The bar arrangement is good for casual meals. Since the galley is a couple of steps down, the cook can enjoy the company of others, and at the same time be out of the main stream of traffic. The engine and generator are under the saloon sole, so if a conventional table was located between the settees, it would be an obstacle for engine maintenance.

Malu Kai is an Irwin 52 ketch designed by Ted Irwin, and built in 1978 in Clearwater, Florida. The hull is fiberglass and the interior is teak over marine plywood. Her main saloon is enormous with a curved couch on the starboard side and two swivel chairs that can face the couch or breakfast bar.

Malu Kai

Stardust

Lusty

MAIN SALOONS

Sayonara is a 118-foot luxury yawl built at Chantier St. Perriere de Lorient in 1968. This highly varnished bar is in the forepeak; an uncommon area for a gathering spot.

Zozo is a 54-foot Taiwan ketch designed by Robert Perry. She is a family liveaboard boat owned by the Magnunssons: Ninni, Hans and their son Joachim. The hull is fiberglass and the interior is teak. The main saloon is on the first level after descending the companionway. (The galley is aft and recessed a couple of steps from the saloon.) The antique coffee table, woven rug, and library give the appearance of a Swedish drawing room.

Sayonara

Zozo

Christiana

WhiteWing

Christiana is a 47-foot double ended gaff ketch built by Colin Archer in the Gregersen yard in Risor, Norway in 1961. The hull is long leaf yellow pine; the interior is African gaboon mahogany. She is owned and operated by Curly Bihun, who takes great pride in classic wooden boats. Here, the main saloon very nicely incorporates the galley and the navigation areas.

White Wing is a 50-foot Alden sloop built in 1938 by J.J. Taylor & Sons in Toronto, Canada. This classic wooden boat is owned and beautifully maintained by Robert Stryker of New Jersey. The interior paneling is stained Mexican mahogany. The main saloon is traditional with leaded glass cabinets and fine cabinetry. The center of the dining table has built in holders for bottles of varying sizes.

Grym III is a 52-foot fiberglass ketch built in 1971 by Frans Maas and designed by Ted Hood. The main saloon is paneled with Honduras mahogany. There is a tidy well organized feeling below. The table is rigged to gimbal one side at a time. Bookshelves, tiles, and a fireplace add a special warmth.

Enchanta's fireplace from the main saloon.(see complete boat on pages 34 - 37).

Grym III

Enchanta

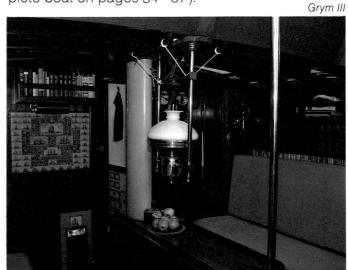

BERTHS AND CABINS

Whatever the size of the boat, if people are going to be sleeping on it with any regularity, there are certain basic requirements for a berth. Occasionally, a yacht broker will try and entice a prospective buyer by pointing out how many bodies the boat can sleep—probably ten, if a few of you sleep on top of the table, in a cupboard, under a shelf, and behind the stove. Realistically, the average adult should have a bunk that is not less than 6'3" (preferably 6'6") long and between 22 inches and 28 inches wide. Aboard a boat there are a variety of berths that can be incorporated: pilot, quarter, doubles, uppers, lowers, pipeberths, settees, V-berths and assorted convertible bunks.

Sleeping needs at sea differ greatly from those in port. Primary attention should be given to sea berths for obvious reasons. We will deal with creature comforts secondarily. Most sailors prefer a fore and aft bunk to one athwartships, because it affords less motion. A four to six-inch-thick polyfoam mattress is better than foam rubber because it will not deteriorate or absorb water. The mattress itself can be covered in any inexpensive material: a domestic cotton or muslin will do. Then, an additional zippered machine-washable fabric: sturdy, colorful cotton or poly/cotton, corduroy or velour. Leather, suede, and velvet require a bit more attention, but can be quite effective. A solid color allows you the prerogative to accent with colorful pillows. Some of the uninitiated may try vinyl, thinking about wet bathing suits or leaking decks when, in fact, vinyl is horrible on a boat. It doesn't breathe, retains heat and moisture or, conversely, stays cold depending upon the climate. Cap moldings to keep mattresses in place and recessed all around toe space are desirable. All sea berths should be equipped with leeboards. Old fashioned wooden ones are all right, but those of canvas are less cumbersome and softer on the hips and shoulders. Ten to twelve inches from the mattress is a good height for a leeboard. An interesting alternative to the conventional leeboard is the adjustable berth. *Concordia*, for example, has a wood-slatted berth, hinged on the hull side and capable of infinite adjustment as to the degree of heel.

Hanging lockers should be long enough for dresses. Also, it is important for lockers to have proper ventilation or louvers to guard against mildew. Drawers that are built under a bunk should extend the maximum depth of the hull, whenever possible. Provision should be made to keep drawers and locker doors from sliding open when the boat is heeled over—either latches or notched runners will work.

Now, that we have covered seaberths and associated topics, we're at liberty to discuss harbor and dockside considerations. A most important aspect to sleeping comfortably in port is proper ventilation. Opening ports, hatches, wind scoops, dorade vents should all be considered carefully to contribute to maximum air flow.

On any liveaboard boat over 35 feet, it is possible to have at least one fixed double bunk. The prospect of converting a dinette to a double every night is not a very happy one. Also a cabin can be created by fitting a double bunk into an alcove with access and privacy curtains.

Cabins need not be dreary places. Bedspreads, pillows and paintings are small, but important, considerations. Fitted sheets save time and effort in maintaining a well-groomed effect, especially in tropical climates where excess bedding is not essential. A private sink or wash basin makes a tremendous difference in the feeling of privacy. A sink can often be rigged to fold up unobtrusively against the bulkhead.

Of course, if it gets too crowded below, you can always sleep on deck!

Sayonara

148

Sayonara

Sayonara is an amazing 118-foot yacht, built in Chantier St. Perriere De Lorient in 1968, remodeled in 1978. She is one of the world's largest and fastest alloy boats. Her interior is paneled in teak, coral wood and ebony. The master stateroom is one of the most impressive cabins we have encountered on a boat. Pictured here are port and starboard views of the aft cabin.

Felicidad

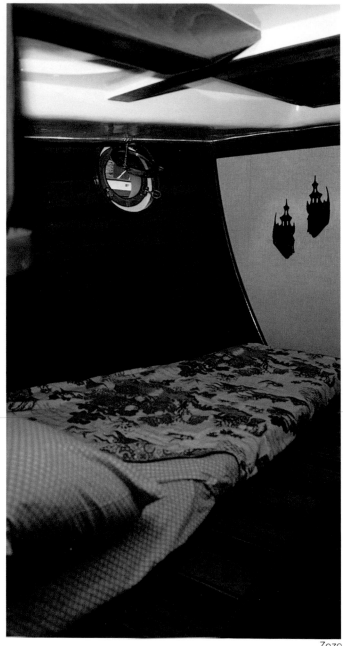

Felicidad is a Doug Peterson 45-foot fiberglass cutter, built in Formosa. Her aft cabin is beam to beam bed. The Browns, who live aboard, think their cabin is spacious, airy and beautiful.

Zozo (featured on page 146) has a forepeak berth that converts to a double by extending the slatted frame.

Zozo

Alegria

Zaida

Quicksilver

Alegria (featured on page 142) shows off her fine craftsmanship with this built in dresser.

Quicksilver (featured on page 144) has spacious, queensize bunks in both port and starboard hulls. Looking through from one end of the boat to the other gives the impression of mirror images.

Zaida, a 1937, 63-foot cutter, designed by John Alden and built by Henry Nevins has a friendly cabin, paneled in butternut and oak. The wicker chairs add a bit of character.

Linda

Eudroma

Sleuth

Eudroma is a 64-foot ketch, (featured on page 134) This cabin features mahogany framed upper and lower bunks.

Vagabond (featured in on page 170) has an aft cabin typical of Taiwan boats, with windows in the transom. There is plenty of space here for both a double and a single bunk.

Linda (featured on page 143) certainly enjoys the use of pillows. This forepeak cabin, carrying on the theme from the main cabin, is replete with them.

Sleuth (featured on page 169) incorporates a block and tackle system on their bunks to compensate for the boat's heel.

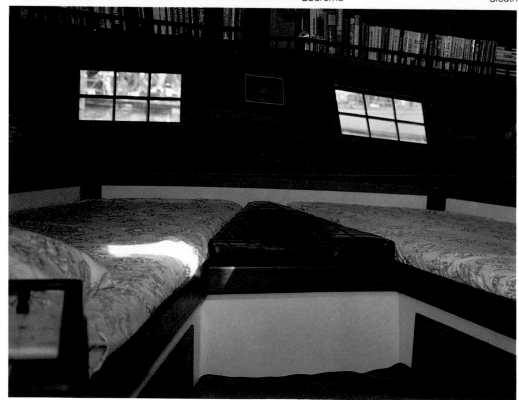

Vagabond

Blue Diamond

Karena

Water Lily

Blue Diamond (featured on page 14) has a charming alcove sleeping area.

Karena, a Morgan 51 has an aft cabin with an athwartship double bunk.

Water Lily is an old-time motorsailer designed by William Hand and built in the Chespeake in 1937. Her hull is pitch pine an oak. This cabin, with its white walls, mahogany trim and oil lamp, is quintessential early 20th Century wooden boat construction.

Scotch Mist (featured on page 98) has two guest cabins port and starboard opposite each other. The one pictured here is deliriously decorated with java-print fabric on the bulkheads that matches the bed-spread; a bit dizzy.

Scotch Mist

HEADS

It's not the bathroom, the john, the W.C., the loo, the powder chamber, the restroom, nor is it *la toilette*. On board a boat, the facility of which we speak is the Head!

Heads are an indelicate subject but important to nautical interiors. We have seen all sorts of heads, from a discreet, portable brass chamber pot (with a lid) to a carpeted, mirrored suite with bathtub, bidet and electroflush...

Cruising boats from about 28 feet and up deserve an enclosed head with enough room to turn around. Likewise, it should not be so open and large that you'll get thrown around in a sea way.

If at all possible, it's hygenic and handy to have a wash basin in the head compartment, as there usually isn't an appropriate spot for toothbrushes next to the galley sink. If the allocated space for the head is too small for a freestanding sink, there are two alternatives. The first is to build a washstand somewhere else less private. The second is to construct a sink in a drawer that pulls out over the toilet with a hose which drains directly into the toilet. We saw this system on the Dutch-built *Contest 33*.

Showers are a civilized addition to the marine head. Even the smallest boats can rig a telephone-type shower head on a flexible hose, with a grating on the sole. Only about four square feet and standing headroom is necessary. It's better to have the sink and the shower drain into a sump tank rather than the bilge.

Stall showers are a luxury. They prevent the toilet paper from getting wet. However, unless your boat is over 50 feet or so, a stall may be a waste of space. Usually a shower curtain can be rigged to prevent water from messing up the entire head. Also, a hose-type shower enables the user to monitor the amount of water output.

Bathtubs are another story. They are truly decadent on a boat, but if you live aboard, are dockside a lot, and water is free, why not? We've seen stainless steel bathtubs, laminated wooden bathtubs, porcelain tubs, tile tubs, and just about every new, large Morgan, Gulfstar, Irwin, etc. has a fiberglass bathtub.

Argyll, a 58-foot yawl, (featured on page 143) has a head with safely rounded edges to go along with the round stainless steel sink. The cabinets are ventilated with a woodwork design, typical of older wooden boats.

Drawers, medicine chests, cabinets, and/or cubbyholes allow certain items to be kept where they belong. It's easier to find tissues, hand lotion, and tweezers in a bin in the head, than to go ferreting through your clothes or the food. Cupboards and drawers should be ventilated and have safety latches. Tiles add a bright touch to the head and are easy to sponge off. An opening porthole is a must in the head. Stick deodorizers work, but a head that is kept fresh daily will not need them. One couple we met built their head out of aromatic cedar! As with other areas of the boat you should stay away from sharp edges. Beveled ones are nicer and less detrimental to your body.

As with any through-hulls, it's better to have seacocks for your inlet and outlet than gate valves. The inlet should be deep enough so that it is still underwater when you heel over, and it shouldn't be too close to the outlet. Another concern is that the rim of the bowl should be several inchs above the waterline to avoid overflow.

A couple aboard a Peter Spronk catamaran in St. Martin had little difficulty with their head since it was simply a hole between the two hulls. This is closer to the origin of the term "head." Historically, the head was a platform with a hole located at the bow of the boat. Today, however, the U.S. Coast Guard would have a few thousand well-chosen words to say about this arrangement.

There are several excellent marine toilet manufacturers, including Wilcox-Crittendon, Baby Blake and La Vac. In general, the more simple and sturdy the unit, the better. It is essential that it can be disassembled easily and reassembled by the plumber aboard. So, carry the rebuilding kits that most of the manufacturers supply.

Eyola

Enchanta

Vanda

Eyola (featured on page 40) has a lovely subdued gray painted head with louvered cabinets.

Enchanta (featured on page 34) has a gracious head with a well-designed cabinet and wash basin.

Vanda (featured on page 128) has a wild blue tiled head. This head contrasts greatly with the rest of the boat which is so traditional.

Mary Day (featured in on page 140) has an "on deck" head. It's a convenient idea for work boats, Baltics and Head Boats.

Mary Day

HEADS

Ysas

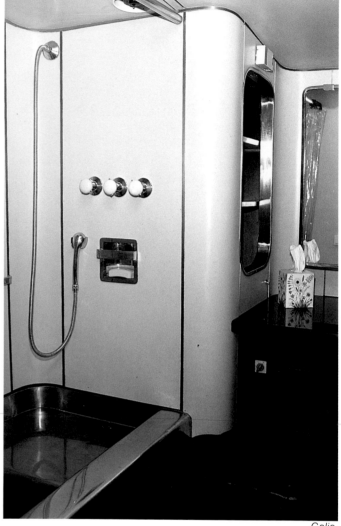

Galia

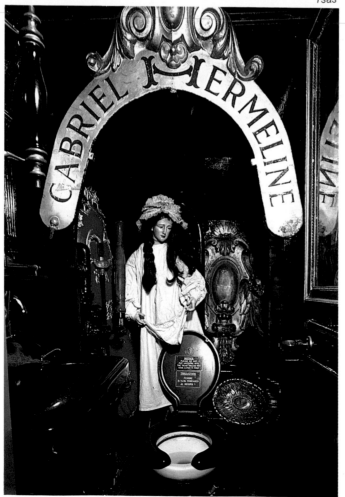

Souqui

Ysas II is a 63 foot Sparkman and Stephens design, de Vries Lentsch built Bermuda ketch. She is owned by a Dutch couple, Dirk and Loes de Jong. This is the master head, with shower, wash basin and ceramic tiled floor and mosaic tiled paneling.

Souqui, the river barge that resides in Paris (featured on page 110) has a most extraordinary head filled with amusements.

Galia (featured on page 48) has an ultra modern head, complete with stainless steel bathtub.

Taipi II

Free Spirit (featured on page 137) has a lovely head with a skylight. There is also a teak grating for the shower.

Taipi II (featured on page 135) has a pristine head that is white and bright, with the basin flush to the counter.

NAVIGATION AREAS AND COCKPITS

We have some general thoughts about cockpits, deckhouses and navigation stations. A cockpit table, either portable or fixed to the binnacle or something else, is practically a necessity for warm weather cruising. Also, a small cockpit locker insulated to act as an icebox is a handy place to store cold drinks and beer. If the galley is located near the companionway, often it is possible to have a pass-through to the cockpit, via a porthole or hatch. Back rests for the helmsman and crew are thoughtful touches. We have seen some angled wooden ones that can be attached to the cockpit coaming.

A deckhouse provides a dry refuge near the cockpit. Designed with settees, it's a pleasant place to have lunch, or just to sit. It's a kind of midway station, a place to take off foul weather gear without disturbing those below. If the boat is long enough to accommodate it, the seats in the deckhouse can be converted to sleeping berths. A proper deckhouse will include a chart table, chart drawers, electronics and stowage space for navigational aids. If the deckhouse is forward of the cockpit, then it is possible to extend its tops and sides to offer some protection to the cockpit.

If the boat has no deckhouse, then the next most logical place for the navigation station is just below the companionway. A separate chart table is desirable as opposed to the dining table so there is never a conflict of interest. Although a quarter berth is often used as the seat for the chart table, a stool or separate seat is better. All the electronics and communication gear as well as navigational aids should be within reach of the navigator.

A locker devoted solely to foul weather gear is a must. It should be at the foot of the companionway, of generous size, well ventilated and self-draining. I've never seen it, but a small hand-held fresh water shower head to wash off the salt would be marvelous. A vent from the engine room (often adjacent) to hasten drying is a nice touch. Also, the entire area around the foot of the companionway should be self draining and covered by grating.

The more cubby holes, small drawers and custom fit racks and holders, the better. A secret place or two built into the cabin to hide valuables is often useful.

Ingenuity and creativity aboard yield great rewards. Details make the difference.

Argyll

Premlata

Premlata

Premalata is a 33-foot Quoddy Pilot, built in Camden, Maine, by Gary Price. Launched in 1975, she was designed by Bob Lane of Friendship, Maine. Her hull is cedar over oak, the deck is Burmese teak; the coaming is long leaf yellow pine. We admired the hatch and the ingenious tiller system whereby a bracket is notched to hold the tiller at any given angle.

Argyll has incorporated a comfortable removable backrest for the cockpit coaming. (see page 143)

Water Lily's pilothouse. (see page 153).

Felicidad, a Peterson 45, (featured on page 150) has the type of navigation station that is self-contained with its own seat, chart table, and electronics at hand.

Windsong

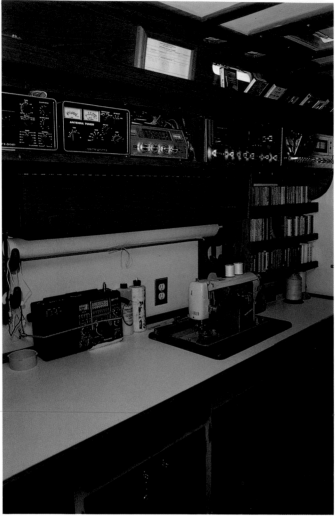

Lusty

Voyager

Windsong is a 58 foot fiberglass ketch, custom built in Skookum, Washington, designed by Ed Monk. This boat was completed in 1980. Her navigation is in the aft cabin. It's often nice to have privacy for some lengthy charting, but for quick checks, the closer to the companionway, the better.

Voyager an Alden Schooner has a well-organized tool cabinet. With this system, there is never any question about where something is when you need it.

Lusty's navigation station is located in the pass-through between the saloon and the aft cabin. The chart table doubles as the workbench. (Lusty is featured on page 145)

Galia (featured on page 48) has a separate navigation room, replete with electronics, and an intercom system to the helsman and foredeck crew. The pull-out bin beneath the navigation table allows the charts to be stowed flat on the diagonal.

Linda, a Baltic trader (featured on page 143) has her navigation station in the deckhouse by the helm. Besides being an efficient location for charting a course, this area is also extemely comfortable.

GALLEYS

Salt air increases the appetite. How many times have you heard that one? Well, it must be true, because meals afloat are invariably tastier than those prepared in the complacency of a kitchen. Man cannot sail on wind alone. Food is fuel for the crew. It follows that a ship's galley is a very important part of a boat. If you have a well-designed galley, then the cook is more apt to prepare meals with love. We have surveyed countless cooks and have come up with both the necessities and the niceties of galley design.

The first consideration is location. We favor aft galleys or if the boat has a center cockpit, an amidships galley works just as well. These two areas tend to provide the cook with a steadier motion under way than a forward galley. Also, being close to the companionway, the cook can benefit from the breeze, and the crew can have ready access to cold drinks and luncheon in the cockpit.

A galley must be well ventilated. Even if the galley is adjacent to the companionway, an overhead hatch and/or opening ports will help keep the cook cool. Nobody wants to—or can—labor lovingly over a *coq au vin* in a steamy little hole.

Many of the older cruising yachts were designed with a forward galley. In the days of paid hands, the owners liked to be separated from food preparation and the crew's quarters. This concept may be just the thing for certain fancy charter yachts, but for those who sail with family and friends, such isolation is not very desirable.

We consider the U-shaped configuration to be the most practical. It affords a compact self-contained unit, apart from the mainstream traffic. While the galley must have ample counter and stowage areas, it is not advantageous to have too large of an open space. Whatever the configuration, provision should be made to keep the cook secure from being tossed around in a lumpy sea.

We have seen galley counters made out of everything from Formica, fiberglass, and stainless steel to butcher block, lineoleum and tile. Butcher block is conventionally constructed out of maple. It is aesthetically pleasing and extremely versatile. Many people object to wooden counters because they think that they absorb odors and are difficult to maintain. If the wood is properly treated, this is not necessarily true. Stainless steel is very easy to keep clean, but tends to scratch. Tiles are better used on vertical surfaces rather than horizontal, as they can catch crumbs in the dividing grooves. Some boats have adopted a new home kitchen device: a

Corning Ware glass substance inlaid in the working area, called a "counter saver." Effective as a hot plate and easy to wipe clean, it doesn't work as a cutting board surface, because it is hard on well honed blades.

Counters at sea require some sort of fiddle system. Removable fiddles tend to collect stuff in the holes from which they are removed. The best fiddles we have seen have open corners for sponging out debris. We also saw one nice butcher block counter with a beveled lip, also for the clean sweep. It is a good idea to avoid any sharp edges on a boat. It is not a good idea to consider the top of your icebox as work space. As soon as you have all of your salad fixings out, and you are chopping away, somebody wants a cold beer. Stove-top cutting boards are likewise problematic. If you are cramped for space, a cutting board designed to fit over the sink is a good alternative. While we are discussing counters, let's discuss wastebaskets. They are inevitable, so you might as well have a built-in container, or frame for your plastic trash bags. The galley is a more pleasant environment with the trash hidden from view. A hole in the counter directly above the wastebasket rids you of scraps with one simple gesture. A basket at the end of a counter can benefit from the same simple sweep, but is not such an appealing sight.

A single sink should be flush with the counter, and large enough to hold a pressure cooker. Sinks are often used under way as a catchall spot for those few items that don't have a permanent home. When you are using your sink as a sink, it's best to have two. You can economize on water by filling one, and using the other for rinsing. Pressure water is convenient, but for long distance cruising, it's essential to have at least one hand or foot pump. There is no question that manual pumps conserve water. It is also a safer bet than a pressure system, should your batteries run down. Besides fresh water, it is also advantageous to have a salt water pump.

We recently saw a very clever idea aboard some new production boats, namely the Swan 55, the Nautical Development Corporation 56, and a custom Gulfstar 50. They had a cabinet which stowed dishes vertically over the sink so that they could be rinsed with a telephone type attachment from the sink and then left to drain without being dried. This time saving system is a fabulous innovation, but we did not encounter the perfect application of it, that is the one where the drippage defied gravity while heeling over. We're convinced that this dish drain and stowage concept can be successfully realized.

This leads us to galley stowage. Cabinets and cubby holes should be partitioned to accommodate both food and utensils. It is so much more pleasant to have all your kitchen gear in sight and readily available, rather than to go digging to the bottom of a pile for it. A separate spice rack, either built in or nailed up, is both useful and attractive. Uniform spice containers assure a tight fit. One boat we saw used hose clamps to contain the spice bottles, allowing for differences in size and width.

The sort of utensils you have is a topic that should be discussed or thought of in conjunction with where they will be stored. Several boats have compartments expressly designed for their plates, bowls, and cutlery. We have seen wedgewood and crystal carefully stowed in a breakfront with drawers that pull out and lock into place (Scotch Mist) We have also seen a silverware drawer (Galia) with a little slot for every knife, fork and grapefruit spoon.

Several more modest arrangements include movable vertical pegs stationed around a stack of plates and compartmentalized Plexiglas or wooden dividers. Wine glasses can be hung bar style by the stem as long as the rack has a slide to secure the glasses from coming out of the slot. Coffee mugs can be hung from hooks as long as the hooks are the kind with a spring steel closure. Copper pots hanging may look pretty in a kitchen, but that system is far too dangerous for a galley. Pots and pans, if they are purchased with any forethought, should nest into one another, with skillets and saucepans sharing interchangeable covers. Random covers that don't fit securely on a pot are a waste of time and space. Kitchen ware sections in department stores, or specialty shops like Pier 1, Pottery Barn, or some other bazaar or boutique have ingenious applications for the boat as well as the home. See through jars with tight fitting caps for flour, sugar, pasta, and other dry goods, are very effective. You can see what quantity you are dealing with, and you don't have to worry about paper or cupboard boxes getting soggy. You don't necessarily have to go to a ship's chandlery, and pay exorbitant prices for nonskid dishes. There are non nautical manufacturers who make dishes and bowls with rubber bottoms (Rosti is one).

Stainless steel is by far the best substance for cookware. We have a prejudice against aluminum (for nutritional not nautical reasons), and copper takes considerable effort to keep shiny. Cast iron, unless well seasoned, rusts, and Teflon doesn't seem to endure. We would also like to put a pitch in for pressure cookers. They are extremely versatile; they can roast, steam, make soups and stews, and

Photograph by Dan Nerney

even bake bread. Dried soybeans, lentils, kidney beans and brown rice can all be prepared in less than half their normal cooking time. Saving energy is always an important consideration on board.

There are many differences of opinion regarding stoves. Unless you relish continual one pot creations, a two burner stove is the minimum requirement on board. It is possible to live without an oven if your space and pocketbook are inflexible. We have experienced all the different cooking methods and have concluded that propane or natural gas is the best. The minute you mention propane, everyone clamors about Coast Guard regulations, fumes in the bilge and boats blowing up. Despite all the hysterical publicity, propane is the cleanest, easiest to use and quickest cooking fuel. Propane must be handled intelligently. The tanks should be mounted on deck or installed in a compartment that is vented to allow any fumes that escape to be carried overboard. Also an ideal valve arrangement is a switch and warning light adjacent to the stove, alerting you if the valve at the tank is open and allowing you to close it from the stove. All lines should be checked for leaks. Copper lines are favored by some, but if you are going to have a gimbaled stove, and you should, a flexible stainless steel hose is better. Gimbaled or not, copper is brittle and may crack. Propane is readily available nearly everywhere.

Natural gas is safer than propane because the fumes are lighter than air. The problems with natural gas are that it is difficult to come by, more fuel is required, and it does not burn as hot as propane. Alcohol is probably the most widely used marine stove. Alcohol is considered to be a "safe fuel" because the fire it creates can be doused with water; which is good because alcohol fires are common. Alcohol stoves tend to be more expensive than propane ones. Alcohol takes a lot of effort to prime, cooks slowly, and is not always available in faraway places.

There are also kerosene stoves. Being a petroleum based fuel, kerosene has impurities. Stove orifices are likely to get clogged up. A few kerosene users complained to us that they must replace their burners every six months. Also several models of kerosene stoves must be primed with alcohol in order to get them hot enough to ignite. Flareups are not infrequent, but of course a practised user will swear that kerosene presents no problem at all.

Diesel stoves tend to be large, heavy, impractical to gimbal and slow to start. However, they deserve consideration for a larger boat that does extensive cold weather cruising since they can produce vast amounts of hot water and use the same fuel as the ships engine.

Electric stoves are out of the question unless you spend a significant time alongside the dock where

Jan Pamela II 1963.141 foot Dutch-built Motor Yacht

Photograph courtesy of Boating

you can plug into shore power. Starting up the generator to brew a cup of coffee or make popcorn at sea is not our idea of convenient! Again we are prejudiced, but we just don't like cooking on electric stoves even in the most elaborate kitchen on shore. We are not against electricity! Electric outlets in the galley are useful for shoreside gadgets such as blenders, beaters and Cuisinarts.

More important than kitchen gadgetry is the refrigeration system in a galley. It used to be the norm to have an old-fashioned icebox aboard a boat. Lugging melting ice down the dock, and draining milky colored water from the ice box every few days is a plague to everyone. We do not believe that a mechanical refrigeration system is a luxury. If you do a fair amount of cruising, the eternal cost of ice and the frequent spoilage of groceries will convince you of the economy of a cold-plate system. Two of the most popular systems are Grunert and Adler-Barbour. Another good system used widely in the Caribbean is Iceberg. The key to effective refrigeration is good insulation. Polyurethane foam is one excellent insulator. For a refrigerator it should be at least two inches thick, for a freezer, four inches should do the trick. A eutectic-holding plate system is the best and the most expensive, costing about $1,000 plus. Running the engine one to two hours a day will cool the holding plates enough to keep the box cold for 24 to 28 hours. Cruising with a lot of friends or a charter party, it is handy to have either a built-in or Igloo type icebox in addition to your mechanical refrigeration. We have seen several coolers built into the cockpit locker with a drain overboard or into the bilge. These are handy for frequent cold drink usage. Also, some mechanical refrigerators on board racing vessels in particular have a beer or soda dispenser at their base—anything to keep those thirsty crew members from opening and shutting the refrigerator all the time.

Top-loading ice boxes or refrigerators are more practical than front-loading ones. Front loaders may make you less nostalgic for the comforts of home, but they lose cold air quickly and are capable of spilling out their contents on a close reach. One particularly effective front-loading system has a series of stainless steel drawers that pull out on a track. This system seems to work fairly well.

In order to make your top loader more palatable to tackle, you should have shelves and bins to separate various items. It is possible to organize your refrigerator so that you don't have to pull every item out to find one thing. Ventilated vegetable bins and net hammocks can hold a lot of bulky onions, potatoes and carrots. The temptation to put simply everything in the refrigerator must be resisted. A carefully planned menu will deplete the perishable items first.

Many of the above tidbits about galleys may seem too banal or self evident to discuss, however we are continually surprised at how few galleys have incorporated even the most common things mentioned above. We have yet to discover the perfect galley.

GALLEYS

Paradise

Paradise, a Gulfstar 50 (featured on page 144) has an L shaped galley separated from but facing the main saloon. There is plenty of counter space, customized dish stowage, and a double stainless steel sink.

Free Spirit (featured on page 137) has the type of galley that would be exceptional even in a home. The butcher block counters are both decorative and functional. The galley is raised so that the cook can see outside. There is a front loading refrigerator and plenty of drawers and cabinet space. A pass-through to the dinette and saloon saves many steps.

Free Spirit

166

Rachel and Ebenezer

Viking

Rachel and Ebenezer is a 105-foot "Down East" Coasting Schooner built in 1975. She operates as a Head Boat in New England and the Caribbean. Her galley sports two stoves in order to accommodate all the charter guests. Beautiful butternut paneling enhances the galley.

Viking is a 40-foot ketch (featured on page 142). Her aft galley uses all available space very efficiently. Spices and condiments are visible and within easy reach. The counters and stove are well fiddled and the cook has a security strap to use at sea. Also note the terrific stainless steel pressure cooker on the stove.

Vixen is a New York 40 (featured on page 144). Her classic galley enjoys a double stainless steel sink, with a cutting board custom made to fit over one half. Her cupboards are well crafted and the counters have safe bevelled edges.

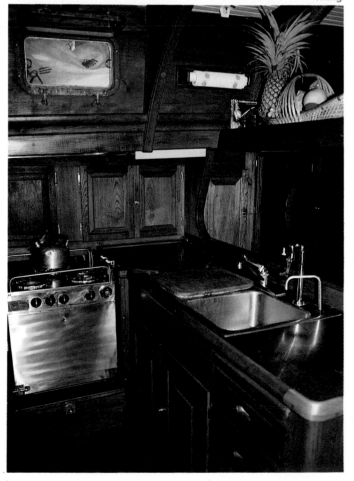

Vixen

GALLEYS

Amoeba is a Peter Noble design, ferrocement schooner, built in Port Cartier, Quebec. Her owner, Roy Bryson, designed her aft saloon/galley arrangement. On the port side is a stainless steel sink, tiled counter, dish stowage, and stove. To starboard is additional workspace, bar, and the refrigerator/freezer. Directly aft of the galley is the dining table and V shaped settee. The combination of galley and saloon pleases the cook providing a congenial culinary environment for her.

Miss Caroline is a Westsail 42-foot Shipmaster, built in California of fiberglass. Her galley is amidships: an attractive space with teak paneling and two portholes. It has a double stainless steel sink, a Crosby 12v cold plate refrigeration system that requires about three hours daily of engine time, and a gimbaled propane stove. There is a special garbage container, and stowage everywhere. There are individual slots for cups, plates and bottles in a built-in unit. A hammock is a colorful sight strung up in an out-of-the-way, but visible, place.

Amoeba

Miss Caroline

Amoeba

Miss Caroline

Sleuth is a 54-foot racing sloop built by Palmer Johnson in Sturgeon Bay, Wisconsin. Her galley is paneled in solid teak. There is a front-loading refrigerator, leaving more counter space. Similar to *Kialoa* there is a separate beer dispenser at the bottom of the unit for thirsty racers. All of the cabinets exhibit fine craftsmanship. Sleuth is owned by Steve and Doris Colgate of Offshore Sailing School. Note the stainless steel steps on either side of the stove which allow Doris to reach the top cabinets.

Aquila, a 42-foot Sparkman & Stephens yawl (featured on pages 6-9) has a lovely galley counter inlaid with colorful Mexican tiles.

Aquila

Sleuth

GALLEYS

Ocean Mistral

Ocean Mistral is an Ocean 60 built by Southern Ocean Shipyard in Poole, England. The galley is aft and is well designed with plenty of surface working area and integral security for the cook. Pulling down the bar above the stove, locks it in and out of gimballed position, thus saving space. The tiles add an attractive touch to the galley.

Vagabond is a 52-foot William Garden ketch built in Taiwan in 1976. She is fiberglass with teak decks and interior. The galley is terrific, compact and secure. The rim around the counter doubles as grab rails. These rails could be improved upon by making the openings flush with the counter to facilitate cleaning.

Vagabond

170

Whistler

Tivoli

Whistler is an Ocean 71, designed by Van de Staadt, and built at Southern Ocean Shipyard in England in 1972. Believe it or not, this galley is the inspiration of Graham Kerr, the Galloping Gourmet, a previous owner. Amply fiddled and generally well laid out with a convenient pass-through to the main saloon, we were somewhat surprised at the shocking blue and the electric stove.

Tivoli is a 71-foot racer/cruiser built by Sangermani in Lavagna, Italy in 1967 and designed by Anselmi Boretti. She is single planked mahogany on Iroko frames, with a teak interior. The galley is forward of the main saloon on the port side. There is an overhead hatch in this otherwise closed compartment; also, plenty of counter space and a little breakfast area for the cook and crew.

Endless Summer is a custom West Indies 46-foot sloop, designed by Charlie Morgan in 1979, and built of fiberglass with a steel frame. Owned by Don and Pat McNair, this galley is designed for maximum security and efficiency. Pat made sure that there was a special container for garbage, and custom cubbies for the Cuisinart and toaster, as well as a bread drawer and a ventilated vegetable bin. The galley is built with a pass-through to the saloon and also convenient to the cockpit. The cat thinks the galley is just fine.

Endless Summer

GALLEYS

Flying Fifty was built by Hugh McLean and Sons at Gourock and Renfrew, Scotland in 1953. She was designed by Uffa Fox. Her hull is composite: iron frames with teak planking. The galley occupies a private space at the foot of the main companionway, to port. This is a charter galley so the cook enjoys her privacy. There is a custom front loading refrigerator that operates only with the a.c. generator. Since the generator is a constant companion, an electric stove is no problem. Tiles enhance the vertical surfaces above the stainless steel sink and the molding. The cook is not very tall, so the skipper has rigged a grating on the galley floor to help her reach the higher shelves. Glass stowage is in the main saloon, separate from the galley.

Flying Fifty

Flying Fifty

Tiara

Wind Dancer

Wind Dancer is a Cherubini 44 (featured on page 137). Her galley is designed for cooking at sea with its U shaped configuration. She has a Taylor kerosene stove. The cabinets are ventilated with cane work and the diagonal opening porthole is designed to remain ajar even under weigh.

Tiara is a 63-foot Motorsailer ketch, designed by Matlock Boat Corp. and built in Stuart, Florida in 1962. Her hull is strip planked mahogany, covered with fiberglass. Most of the interior is teak. She is owned by Peter and Margaret Stahmer. The galley is done in Formica. A generator is needed to keep the electric stove operating. Margaret likes to keep everything out and accessible. There is even a private corner to sit and have a cup of coffee.

Impulsive is an Irwin 52, built in Clearwater, Florida. Ted Irwin has created a proper galley; it's conveniently located at the foot of the companionway, but to starboard and down a few steps for security. This U-shape yields ample working space, yet is safer for the cook in a seaway than more open or larger galleys.

Impulsive

GALLEYS

Galadriel

Galadriel

Galadriel is a 37-foot steel cruising boat, owned by Heidi and Larry Sorensen of Kirkland, Washington. She was built in Holland, designed by Moerman, in 1956. The galley, like the rest of the boat, has a homespun charm. Heidi likes everything to be stowed in plain sight and uses lots of jars for her drygoods. The wooden goblets, stowed by their stems, drain into the sink. With only a two burner gas stove, Heidi has mastered the art of baking bread in a cast iron frying pan. The galley sole has a slot in it to accommodate the pedestal of a stool which doubles as a navigator's stool. *Galadriel* is not fancy, but delightful and efficient.

Riki Tiki Tavi is a 30-foot New Zealand Cutter built in 1963 of teak on oak. Her galley is quite small, but incorporates clever ideas. This spice rack was created with the use of water hose clamps.

Riki Tiki Tavi

Adventure (featured on page 139) has a galley that resembles a great country kitchen, with its cast iron wood-burning stove, brass water pump, and pots and pans hanging everywhere. Besides being a visual delight, this galley is also utilitarian.

Amigo is a 54-foot custom yawl built by Ditmar and Donaldson in Costa Mesa, California in 1957 of Honduras mahogany over oak. She is owned by John and Gayle Boggs. The galley is L-shaped with a hinged cutting board which, when raised, adds much counter space and changes the galley to a "U".

Leander

Leander is a 39-foot Casey cutter, built in 1947 of mahogany on oak. this wood burning stove adds a great deal of warmth and ambiance to the galley.

Slipaway is a 28-foot Bahamian sloop renovated in 1976 by William and Deborah Pringle. Her hull is pine on horseflesh with a cypress deck. That's right, horseflesh, a common method of laying up a hull in Andros. This kettle in a bucket with lead weights and a primus stove is the system that keeps the Pringle family of four fed aboard *Slipaway*.

Zingara

MYA

Zingara is a 30 foot teak cutter, designed by T. Harrison Butler and built by Moody & Sons in 1935 in Southampton, England. Bruce and Karen Ray of Oxford, Maryland live aboard. The galley is tiny, but efficient and we love brass kettle!

MYA is a lovely, 50-foot schooner, built by Howland and Hunt of Concordia in Ducksbury Shipyard in 1939. Her hull is Honduras mahogany over white oak frames. She is owned by Mathew and Martha Stackpole. Her galley is quite small, but has a place for everything as well as easy access to the cockpit.

Elinor, the Baltic trader (featured on page 138), has a fabulous "on deck" galley, perfect for a boat of her size and nature. It's great cooking, with plenty of fresh air around. The stainless steel counter is easy to keep hygienic and the sink is flush to the counter, so that a grand sweep is uninterrupted.

Elinor